TABLE OF CONTENTS

DEMENTIA GUIDE FOR CAREGIVERS

Everything You Need to Know to Help Your Parents and Yourself

Reysa Manible

Introduction

We remember their love when they can no longer remember.

–Anonymous

Being the person that everyone tends to depend on is a hard thing, no matter how willing someone is to help. As primary caregivers for relatives or parents living with dementia, we cope with a lot of pressure. Oh, and don't get me started on the guilt that manages to hang over us when we battle to balance everything. This seems to intensify with every attempt to juggle caregiving responsibilities with personal and professional lives. Not only that but there's also a large chunk of financial tension that comes with caring for someone with dementia. The medical needs, services, and attention that people with dementia have constantly demand effort and input. It can all get overwhelming, but what else can be done when all we want is to ensure that the people we love feel our affection and care?

Caring for our elderly parents is the beautiful gift we give to them for taking care of us when we were young. Parents with dementia are at their most vulnerable; the love and trust they have for us are what motivates us to walk them through this challenging time. Now, we are responsible for helping with medications, grocery shopping, doctor's visits, and other activities of daily living. Sounds like a hard and scary task, and it is. Caring for elderly parents with dementia is far from easy or simple. Like most things, there are good days and bad. It can also get difficult to lead with empathy, but that is what's required. The aim for any son or daughter of a parent with dementia is to keep them comfortable and feeling safe at this stage of their lives. Though providing this care can be daunting, it will always be worth it to help your loved ones.

You are more than capable of providing care for your parents during this challenging stage of their lives, even if the situation can sometimes feel frustrating. You may even be tired of hearing about how "strong" you are for bearing the load of caring for your loved ones. Cliched advice like, "Take care of yourself" and, "Stay positive" may be the last thing you want to hear. Good thing you're reading this as, although these are all true perspectives, you may be ready to receive some practical guidance on how you can overcome caregiver fatigue, care for yourself, and balance your responsibilities. This book intends to provide you with the tools you need to succeed at caring for your elderly parents as they navigate living with dementia. You will learn strategies and gain knowledge that you can implement to offer high-quality care without losing yourself. By following practical guidance on matters of self-care, you'll be able to manage your physical and emotional health through the process. This will lead to positive interactions between yourself, your parents, service providers, and other family members. Your health will improve as you gain resilience by knowing how to effectively face the obstacles that come with dementia care. This book will help you demystify dementia, understand the behaviors associated with it, provide compassionate care, and navigate the financial landscape of dementia care along so much more! So stick around, you never know how much of this information you need to take home with you.

CHAPTER 1

Dementia Demystified—An Introduction

One person caring about another represents life's greatest value.

–Jim Rohn

Any person providing dementia care for loved ones is fully aware of the sacrifices and difficulties involved. Dementia is not one specific illness. Instead, it is a term that describes multiple symptoms associated with a range of neurological issues that impact the capacity to think and draw from memory. Several diseases form a collective under the umbrella of dementia—all due to abnormal brain alterations that interfere with cognitive performance. Abnormal brain alterations trigger a downward spiral that slows thinking abilities, this eventually impacts behavior, emotions, and interpersonal relations.

Supporting someone with any form of dementia can be hard on the caregiver. Hopefully, learning what dementia is will help avoid some pitfalls that are typically linked to this type of care. This chapter delves into the concept of dementia and highlights the various causes of it. The information here also unpacks the types of dementia that people can experience. When you have a clearer understanding of the term, it will offer new insights on how you can help someone who's dealing with the decline.

Understanding Dementia: An Overview

Dementia is a common medical term used to refer to a loss of cognitive functioning in areas associated with memory, language, problem-solving, and critical thinking abilities Generally, the loss of neural function experienced by dementia patients is sufficient to disrupt an individual's capacity to manage daily responsibilities. Historically, dementia was inaccurately believed to be a normal part of aging. It was referred to as "senile dementia" to support the idea that a severe reduction in cognitive abilities was bound to happen to everyone as they age (*What is Dementia,* n.d.). However, dementia is not a symptom of "old age," so not everyone will experience it. Also, the degrees and symptoms of dementia differ depending on the person and cause of their condition.

Causes of Dementia

Potential causes of dementia are linked to multiple risk factors; some can be changed and others can't (Mayo Clinic Staff, 2023). Lifestyle choices can also contribute to the development of dementia in people.

Unchangeable Causes

- Age

  - People over the age of 65 have a higher risk.

  - Younger people with poor life choices can get it too.

- Genetic influences and history

- A history of dementia in the bloodline increases a person's risk.

    - People without a history can also be affected.

- Down syndrome

    - Issues with brain development associated with this syndrome increase the risk of dementia.

    - By middle age, people are at risk of early-onset dementia.

Preventable Causes

- Lifestyle choices

Poor dietary practices increase the risk of:

- large consumption of alcohol and other substances

- high cholesterol

- fat buildup

- smoking

- limited social participation

- low nutrient and vitamin intake

Lack of physical exercise increases the risk:

- obesity

- no cardiovascular training

- Environmental factors

    - Air pollution

- o   Accident-related brain injury

- o   Lack of sleep

- o   Depression

- o   Use of certain medicines

It's not easy to tell how and when a person can be affected by these risk factors. Consequently, no one but a professional can say for sure when these symptoms cause dementia.

Getting Diagnosed With Dementia

Though memory loss is the core symptom of dementia, experiencing this impairment doesn't automatically indicate that someone has the condition. To be fully certain that your loved one is experiencing early-onset dementia, you need to get a medical diagnosis. You should never just assume that someone's symptoms correlate with the conditions, or conclude that they have the condition without a professional assessment.

Different Types of Dementia

Dementia that's left unmanaged can progress and worsen over time. Once someone is diagnosed with the following types of dementia, it's usually hard to control the symptoms.

Alzheimer's Disease

Alzheimer's is the most prevalent type of dementia, and it accounts for 60–80% of cases (What is Dementia, n.d.). Not all causes of Alzheimer's have been discovered yet, but it seems a small percentage of cases are genetic and passed down from parent to child (Mayo Clinic Staff, 2023). Alternatively, Alzheimer's is caused by clumps of protein accumulating in the brain causing tangles. This progressively begins to damage healthy brain cells, tissue, and connecting fibers. People who are 65 years and older are generally said to be the most vulnerable to getting the diagnosis. But remember, Alzheimer's is not an expected part of the aging process. Depending on exposure to risk factors, it can also impact people who are younger than 65. Though people can live for at least 20 years after the diagnosis, even late diagnosis can reduce life expectancy.

Alzheimer's can't be cured, but it can be treated (What is Alzheimer's Disease, n.d.). The U.S. Food and Drug Administration (FDA) has approved Aduhelm® and Leqembi® as treatments for this condition. Aduhelm®—also referred to as aducanumab—is the first therapy to remove some of the protein clumps in the brain allowing for an improvement in cognitive functioning. Leqembi®, also known as lecanemab, is an antibody that targets the protein responsible for the condition. Both these treatments are said to have good odds of reducing Alzheimer's symptoms. However, it's important to discuss viable options with your doctor to ensure that the benefits of certain treatments outweigh the risks.

Vascular Dementia

The second most prevalent type of dementia is vascular. Microscopic bleeding, oxygen deprivation, and the restriction of blood flow due to vessel blockage in the brain are the main causes (Vascular Dementia, n.d.). Changes in cognition can happen instantly after a stroke, or they can begin gradually as mild symptoms of dementia. Only an estimated 5–10% of people are diagnosed with this type of dementia. For the most part, vascular dementia remains underdiagnosed even with symptoms that are identical to those generally associated with dementia. Some symptoms of vascular dementia include physical ailments commonly linked to a stroke, troubles with speech, lack of balance, and physiological numbness.

Strokes tend to be the common cause of vascular dementia because these affect blood flow and impair nerves within the brain. When the brain is impacted, it causes damage and accelerates changes in cognition, judgment, and attention deficits. MRI tests need to be done to confirm any vascular dementia in a person. Since that type of dementia commonly goes undiagnosed, it's important to get professional screening to look at brain activity and spot any changes.

Frontotemporal Dementia

This type of dementia is usually due to a disconnection of neural nerves in the frontal and temporal lobes of the brain (Mayo Clinic Staff, 2023). These impairments are evident in the person's inability to think, reason, communicate, and interact in familiar environments. The damage to the frontal and temporal lobes makes it harder to undertake normal processes.

Lewy Body Dementia

Ballon-like clumps of protein in the brain are known as Lewy bodies (Mayo Clinic Staff, 2023). People with Alzheimer's and Parkinson's disease commonly have these clumps. Additionally, Lewy body dementia is commonly recognized and diagnosed. Its symptoms include visual hallucinations, poor focus, tremors, and physical stiffness.

Mixed Dementia

As the name implies, "mixed" dementia describes brain changes that cause a person to experience a combination of dementia types simultaneously. Typically, people will show mixed symptoms of Alzheimer's, vascular, and Lewy body dementia—more common in people over the age of 80 (Mayo Clinic Staff, 2023).

Plenty of other illnesses—like thyroid functioning and vitamin deficits—can cause cognitive impairments that aren't necessarily described as dementia.

Signs and Symptoms of Dementia

Different cognitive and psychological changes are typically associated with dementia-related memory loss (Mayo Clinic Staff, 2023). Some of these symptoms include:

- Cognitive changes
  - Loss of memory
  - Forgetfulness
    - sudden challenges with communication or finding words
    - confusion
    - disorientation
  - Visual and spatial impairments
  - Issues with reasoning
  - Problems with planning and organization
  - Poor motor control
  - Lack of coordination
  - Problem-solving issues

- o Repeating questions
  - o Trouble with performance and completing complex tasks
- Psychological changes
  - o Unexplained changes in personality
  - o Irritability
  - o Depression
  - o Anxiety
  - o Uncharacteristic and inappropriate behavior
  - o Possible hallucinations
  - o Possible paranoia

It's important to get your family doctor or a specialist on board when you start to see early signs of dementia in someone you know. Including medical personnel in decisions can be vital in helping you manage the progression and symptoms.

The Progression of Dementia

All types of dementia are progressive; the treatments that people get can slow progression down but not stop it. The severity and experience of dementia range from the mildest form—which impacts someone's functioning in minor ways but doesn't necessarily stop it entirely—to the severe form. In the most severe stage, people with the diagnosis can become completely dependent on external assistance to carry out normal functions such as eating, going places, and remembering things.

The progression of dementia increases the need for dementia care and support.

Stages of Dementia

The stages of dementia's progression are categorized as early, middle, and late dementia. The three categorizations represent the mild, moderate, and severe forms of dementia symptoms. You can use these stages to help you understand how dementia can progress over time.

Early or Mild

Early dementia can last for about two years before the symptoms worsen and start to affect daily functioning (The Progression and Stages of Dementia, 2020). The symptoms of early-onset dementia aren't typically noticeable at first and can include:

- Memory problems
    - Forgetting events
    - Confabulations (unintentional false memories that could be totally fictive or include combinations of fragments of real past events)
    - Losing or misplacing items
- Difficulties planning or thinking things through
    - Impulsivity
    - Confusion
    - Indecision
- Mood alterations

- o   Sadness

  - o   Frustration

  - o   Agitation

- Visual impairments

  - o   Misjudging the distance

  - o   Seeing things that aren't there

Of course, these symptoms may not be alarming in the beginning because they may not happen as frequently as in other stages. Many people at this stage tend to need minimal assistance with daily tasks but maintain their independence for the most part. During this stage, it's important to encourage the person to continue doing what they can do without imposing your fears and expectations on them. Rather than taking over their lives, only provide help in places where you can see that the person is struggling. You can also help by setting reminders, creating schedules, and using prompts to encourage collaboration between them and yourself. Taking over tasks can frustrate a person with early dementia and threaten their feeling of independence. This stage is also when people should start planning the next steps in case the disease becomes more severe.

Moderate

As the dementia progresses to the middle stage, the person will start to need persistent reminders. The symptoms experienced in the early stage will also start occurring more often. Moderate dementia is when you usually begin to develop a sense of urgency about the slight concerns that built up within you over the weeks. During this time, the person will require a bit more focused care to cope with daily demands. Memory loss symptoms at this stage worsen to the point where the person may need to be reminded to care for themselves. For example, laying their clothes out for them can remind them to dress themselves while starting the water can prompt washing. Symptoms of moderate dementia typically include:

- Worse memory issues
    - Inability to recognize familiar people
    - Confusing strangers with family or friends
    - Battling to remember new information
    - Repetitive speech or questioning
- Difficulties with the use of language
    - Challenges finding the right words
    - Forgetting the point mid-sentence
    - Inability to follow what someone else is communicating
- Challenges with orientation
    - Confusion about the time of day
    - Feeling unsure about where they are, even in familiar environments
    - Forgetting the direction to home
- Restlessness
    - Fidgeting

- o   Pacing (walking up and down)

  - o   Trailing or following the caregiver aimlessly

- Behavioral changes

  - o   Shouting

  - o   Aggression

  - o   Repeating inappropriate behaviors

- Delusions

  - o   Believing untrue things

  - o   Suspecting people for no reason

- Paranoia

  - o   Always on guard

  - o   Believing that people, even loved ones, are plotting their downfall

This is usually the stage where dementia care may require more than one person. At this stage, it may be beneficial to have paid care or be prepared to commit more hours of your day to supervising dementia care. A person in the middle stage of dementia may feel all emotions strongly and switch between them easily. They can go from feeling afraid to feeling angry or sad in an instant.

Late or Severe

Now, this part is tough. At the severe stage of dementia, people can go from calmness and confusion to being frazzled and inconsolable. Late dementia is when a person experiences symptoms intensely including:

- Memory and language impairments
    - Struggle to remember events (time shifting)
        - for example, asking about a loved one who passed
    - Stop recognizing places entirely
    - Difficulty remembering what objects are used for
    - May not recognize themselves in the mirror
    - Forgetting how to speak a language
    - Understanding very little communication or responding to nothing at all
    - Limited to no use of words
- Behavioral and physical challenges
    - Falling more frequently
    - Feeling unsafe
    - Being aggressive
    - Difficult or painful swallowing (dysphagia)
    - Losing control of bowels and bladder

The late stage will require full-time care, and it's usually the shortest stage of the condition stretching between one and two years (The Progression and Stages of Dementia, 2020). Severe dementia is hard to miss because of the turmoil that usually happens during that period.

Knowing these stages is essential because they can guide you to know what types of behaviors and emotional responses to prepare for. Of course, you can never be fully ready for the type of adjustments you need to make in your life because of dementia care. Also, it is not guaranteed that dementia will follow these exact stages of progressions; people will have unique experiences of the condition. Though it's natural to want to know which stage of progression someone is in, it's more important to approach this diagnosis one step at a time. Take each day as it unfolds for you, as it's the best way to prevent feeling overwhelmed.

Why Dementia Progresses

Multiple types of dementia can progress when the damage in the brain spreads to multiple areas. As time goes by, it gets harder for the brain to manage the alterations; eventually, normal functioning is lost. With progression, parts of the brain become so badly damaged that nothing can be done to manage behaviors, emotions, and other physical responses.

Common Misconceptions About Dementia

Approximately 5.8 million older adults at the age of 65 or older have dementia in the US (Newman, 2020). Experts in the field predict that twice as many people will be affected by the year 2050. No wonder the idea of dementia has sparked widespread fears linked to a range of misconceptions. Demystifying dementia means busting some of the myths about the condition that have developed over the years.

Myth One: Dementia Is an Inevitable Part of Aging

This is a lie, dementia is not an inevitable part of aging. Only about 3% of people between 65 and 75 years old are diagnosed with the most common form of dementia in the US (Newman, 2020). Additionally, the risk of diagnosis sits at 17% and 32% for people aged 75 to 84 years and older than 85, respectively. These statistics aren't significant enough within each elderly category to conclude that dementia is inevitable with age. If it were inevitable, everyone would be guaranteed to get dementia as soon as they turn 65 or older.

Myth Two: Dementia and Alzheimer's Are Interchangeable Terms

As you know, dementia describes a collective of memory loss illnesses, and Alzheimer's is included in that group. So no, these terms can't be interchangeable because the latter is the experience of mental ailments, while the former is an umbrella term under which the latter falls.

Myth Three: Only The Elderly Can Get Dementia

This is not true because young people can also get dementia. Though age is a risk factor—the older you get the higher the chances of acquiring the disease—it's not a determinant. Young people between the ages of 30 and 64 years have a 0.26% chance of succumbing to early-onset dementia (Newman, 2020). This percentage increases to 0.4% for the older group of young people aged between 55 and 64 years.

Myth Four: Aluminum Pans Can Cause Dementia

Research hasn't found a connection between aluminum and dementia. If anything, studies suggest that less than 1% of aluminum present in food and drinks is absorbed in the body, as it is not easily absorbable (Newman, 2020). Nonetheless, the absorbed aluminum is quickly processed and cleared out through the kidneys.

Myth Five: Dementia Signifies The End of Life

Getting an early diagnosis of dementia can be helpful, so don't be afraid. Many people still live healthy, active lives despite being diagnosed with the condition. Though progression increases the likelihood of lifestyle changes, it doesn't mean someone with dementia stops living a satisfying life.

Hopefully, after this round of myth-busting you feel incentivized to do more research on the topic before you get yourself into a panic about things that aren't true. Now that we've unpacked some information to improve your understanding of dementia, prepare to gain more knowledge about the behaviors associated with the condition. This topic is to be addressed in the next chapter.

CHAPTER 2

Deciphering Dementia Behavior

None of us wants to be reminded that dementia is random, relentless, and frighteningly common.

–Laurie Graham

As dementia progresses, a person might start to respond to situations in ways that are hard to understand. The behavioral changes associated with dementia are probably one of the most difficult aspects that both the caregiver and patient struggle with. When a person with dementia starts to act uncharacteristically, it's usually the beginning of a tough road ahead.

However, behavioral changes aren't always directly caused by dementia itself. People experience changes for other reasons including fear, frustration, and the environment they're exposed to. For instance, someone may behave out of fear from the thought of a future with dementia in it. They could feel frustrated by the fact that the condition is making it harder for them to remember certain things. People may even change how they behave because of the environment; for example, they may be tired of the lack of mistrust around their ability to care for themselves. Essentially, behavioral changes can be connected to internal aspects that aren't necessarily due to dementia.

So it's important to listen and consider other reasons for behavioral changes during this time. Allowing yourself to be open-minded to multiple possibilities will help you learn information about the person to improve how you care for them. The main point of this chapter is to guide your understanding of dementia behaviors so you can handle tough moments with compassion. By the end of this chapter, you will be able to respond properly to different behaviors shown by your loved ones.

Understanding Dementia Behavior

Dementia can influence changes in behavior, personality, and decisions. For example, people who receive a dementia diagnosis can easily find themselves losing interest in activities they used to find joy in. A lot of the time behaviors feel challenging for people with dementia. It's almost an obstacle that makes it much more difficult for them to continue normal interactions and routines. By understanding the behaviors associated with each stage of dementia you can be a huge benefit in the field of dementia care. It's essential to keep at the forefront of your mind that the person is not intentionally trying to make it hard for you to care for them. This condition is truly one of the hardest to deal with because the patients themselves can't control what they will or won't do next. Imagine how lonely it must feel to slowly lose grasp of your personality and the reality around you; that's what dementia does to someone over time. Hopefully knowing this builds some warmth and softness within you that can empower you to lead with kindness instead of responding to the dementia behaviors with frustration. The behaviors that you can expect from people living with dementia are as follows:

- Hoarding

- Repetition

- Wandering

- Agitation

- Aggression

- Memory loss

- Confusion

- Sleep issues

Of course, how people experience dementia will be different so the manifestations won't always be the same between people. The characteristics or types of dementia behaviors will be explored next.

Hoarding in Dementia

People with dementia might hide, lose, or hoard things for long periods. Losing things is more related to the dementia symptom of memory loss. When things are misplaced, it can be frustrating for someone with dementia and might also ignite some delusions. For example, someone who starts losing things more than normal may begin to convince themselves that someone is stealing things from them. Though you might know that this thought is not true, a person with dementia could feel like there's no other way to rationalize the losses. Delusional thinking can catapult into hiding and hoarding behavior in dementia.

Causes of Hoarding

Typically, people with dementia are motivated to keep things in an attempt to protect what they care about. However, this can be excessive and result in hoarding. In fact, many reasons are tied to hoarding behavior.

Isolation

When someone feels alone they may shift their focus to hoarding in an attempt to feel some sort of importance. The need to hoard valuables is a common response to loneliness.

Clinging to Memories

The desire to hold onto what seems to be slipping away is great motivation for hoarding. Also, things that happen daily can trigger memories of the past where there was a lack in some capacity, hence, making someone want to secure themselves against that. For example, a memory of a sibling taking away their clothes may be triggered during dementia, consequently resulting in the belief that hiding and hoarding clothes is a necessity to prevent history from repeating itself.

Loss

Dementia causes people to slowly lose parts of their character. Memories, normal routines, relationships, finances, and other meaningful connections often come under attack when someone is battling dementia. The feeling of loss can stimulate the need to safely keep things just to maintain some sort of control over what stays. In a state where everything feels so unstable and fleeting, the need to hoard can increase.

Fear

Naturally, the delusion and paranoia associated with further stages of dementia can result in false realities. Someone with dementia may believe that people don't want them to have nice things, so they may hide and hoard in an attempt to combat the idea that someone is coming to take their things away.

The causes of hoarding don't need to make sense, they need only to be respected. Dealing with dementia is difficult enough without being confronted with the truth of how far out of touch one is with reality. It's important to do things that help people manage hoarding rather than force them to change it.

Managing Hoarding and Hiding

Hiding can happen when a person believes that something is meant to be somewhere it's not. A person may believe that they left an item somewhere close to them even if they haven't. When this occurs, it's important to attempt and see things from the patient's viewpoint. Trying to change the perspective of someone with dementia is a futile and frustrating exercise for both you and the person. Playing to the reality that a person with dementia believes can help calm them in moments of panic, thus, allowing you to provide better dementia care.

Alternatively, hoarding can happen as a defense mechanism to losing things. Someone with dementia may want to keep as many items as possible as a way to maintain control in a situation where they feel a lack of it. So, they might stockpile things in an attempt to hold on to a life that they can feel is slipping away. When this happens, it's important to approach it with utmost care. Don't dismiss the person's experience because you don't understand it. To try and cope with hoarding behaviors without throwing things away, you can ensure that you leave a dementia patient's area as tidy as possible while respecting all of their stuff.

Consider keeping letters, images, and posts in marked trays. Preserve anything important to the person you're caring for because that will help them keep their mental peace. You can even consider using technology such as locator devices to help the person keep track of the items that they are most accustomed to losing. Also, if the person you're caring for leaves an item in a place that doesn't pose a risk to anyone, it would be better to leave it there for them. Dementia care is not about taking over someone's life but supporting them through it. So, be mindful and thoughtful when approaching all dementia behaviors.

Repetitive Behavior in Dementia

Another common behavior when it comes to dementia is repetitive actions. People with dementia tend to repeat the same activities, gestures, speech, sounds, and questions. Repetitive behavior is commonly caused by loss of memory, so someone may say something and forget that they did. A person may, for example, keep checking where they left their keys and wallet or opening their fridge only to forget what they were looking for.

Typically, when someone is repeating behavior it's better to respond to them from an emotional position rather than a logical one. You may feel tempted to point out the person's mistake or repetitive behavior to them but refrain from it. Instead, choose to support them by listening to each repetition as though it's being said for the first time. Dementia care requires you to be a source of comfort and security for the people who are going through the experience. Caring for someone with dementia is about putting your frustrations aside to be present with someone during their time of need. In other words, do what you can to ensure that the person feels reassured even as they experience confusion. For example, if they keep looking for something you can reassure them by pointing to the thing instead of getting upset that they keep circling back and forth.

Managing Repetitive Behaviors

To help someone manage repetitive behaviors you need to be patient and keep calm. Your tone and choice of words when dealing with repetitive behavior need to be kind at all times. Though frustration may threaten to be your first response, it's important to remember that no one chooses to have dementia; hence, being gracious in how you respond will go a long way.

In addition to patience, you also need to put tools in place to promote some sense of normality. For example, if someone is at the stage of forgetting a family member, then keep a picture of them close by to keep reminding them of who the person is. Be practical with your solutions to provide support in a non-invasive manner. Another example of this is to consider placing a calendar nearby for someone who tends to repeatedly ask about the date. This way, you can continue to scratch through the calendar to represent each passing day.

At the core of managing repetitive behavior is also considering what desire may be motivating the behavior. Repetition is usually tied to some desire, and finding out what that is will help you become a better caregiver. For instance, someone who's constantly asking about the grocery store may do so out of fear that the food will run out. The best course of action is reassurance and a reminder that the food is taken care of. Fear is usually at the root of most dementia behaviors; once you understand that, you will start to manage behaviors better.

You can also engage the person who has repetitive behaviors in an activity that they enjoy doing. This usually helps them to shift their focus to something more positive and fun. Sometimes repetitive actions can seem motivated by anxiety; for example, someone may pace around the room or prod and pull at things around them. If this is the case, perhaps providing the person with tools to cope with this anxiety may be helpful. Depending on what works for the person, you can offer soft items to fidget with, warm blankets, and even some music. Sensory stimulation—especially acoustic—typically calms dementia patients because music is the one thing that effortlessly connects everyone.

Wandering in Dementia

Wandering is another behavior that's associated with dementia, and it's quite common. This is the process of walking away from familiarity in a state of confusion or aimless searching. Failing memory and a decline in cognitive abilities may make it hard for someone with dementia to remember or explain why they've wandered.

Causes of Wandering

Some wandering can be caused by memory loss. For example, someone could start walking and forget where they were trying to go. Besides loss of memory, reasons for wandering can also include:

- Excess energy and restlessness

- Confusion

- Discomfort

- Change in environment

- Boredom

- Search of the past

- Believing there's somewhere else they should be

All wandering is person-dependent, meaning all people will have unique reasons for wandering. This is a challenging behavior to try to account and prepare for, however, there are things you can do to try to cope with it.

Managing Wandering

If you're concerned about someone's safety when it comes to this behavior, it's important to have an action plan for it. In this plan, you need to have emergency contacts written down along with a list of places that person is likely to go. Also, make it your priority to remember what the person is wearing daily, so you can describe to the police what to look for in the event of a search. Including neighbors and other trusted community people in this action plan can also put you at ease when wandering happens.

Additionally, you can manage wandering by proactively identifying whether any illnesses, medication, or discomfort triggered it. Get your doctor involved in assessing the symptoms and possible causes of the behavior so you can get some medical insight into it. Keep an open mind to possible psychological causes that may have influenced the behavior as well such as anxiety, clouded judgment, and depression. Knowing what motivated the wandering can help prevent or prepare for the possibility of it happening again. If wandering becomes frequent, it may be good to consider having the person keep an identification card on them.

Responding to Agitation and Aggression

According to Carrarini et al. (2021), aggressive and irritable behaviors are observed in about 70% of people who experience cognitive decline from dementia. After apathy and depression, agitation is the third most common symptom of dementia. Dementia behavior can also be characterized by agitation and aggression, these are two experiences that are typically consequences of emotional distress. This distress harms cognitive performance, functioning, and a person's quality of life.

Causes of Agitation and Aggression

A variety of reasons can explain agitation and aggression in dementia including:

- Unfamiliar people and environments

- Changes in routine and structure

- Feeling unsafe, anxious, and threatened

- Tiredness and fear

- Overstimulation from technology and devices that can make it difficult to understand the world

- Complex routines

Managing Agitation and Aggression

Several studies, including those reported by Carrarini et al. (2021), have explored non-pharmaceutical approaches to managing agitation and aggression in dementia including:

- Tailored care

  - o Providing custom care to someone with dementia ensures that their symptoms are treated as unique which is likely to help them more appropriately.

  - o Person-centered care (PCC) takes into account a person's history, social background, personality, and lifestyle to provide a positive structure tailored to their needs.

- Music therapy

  - o Music can reduce agitation in dementia patients, the frequency of most sounds is associated with calming tones which improve these behaviors.

  - o White noise is known to reduce sundown syndrome i.e., sundowning—the augmentation of the neuropsychiatric symptoms like agitation, aggression, and confusion in the late afternoon, evening, or at night—allowing for better sleep at night and less agitation during the day.

  - o Create a personalized playlist to help the person make positive associations throughout the day using music.

- Increase daytime activity

  - o Having multiple fun things to do during the day is known to reduce boredom, therefore, it reduces the possibility of agitated behaviors.

- o Introduce cognitively stimulating tasks such as reading, socializing, and completing tasks.

  - o Socialization is known to improve aggression and agitation because a person gets to build healthy connections and feel secure.

- Create calm surroundings

  - o Remove loud noises

  - o Avoid stressors

  - o Prioritize rest and privacy

  - o Simplify tasks

- Respond calmly

  - o Ask for permission to touch or move things.

  - o Use calm, reassuring, and positive statements to provide support:

    - ▪ "Can I help you?"

    - ▪ "You are safe here."

    - ▪ "I'm sorry that you feel upset, I know this is hard."

    - ▪ "I will stay here until you feel better."

  - o Listen and understand the reasons for the person's agitation.

o Check in on your own emotions to prevent reacting from personal frustration.

Of course, whether certain interventions are useful or not will be determined by what the individual needs. Some people may have instant improvements from PCC while others may not. All dementia care should be looked at from an individual approach because everyone being treated is different and might have unique requirements. Often, having a team of healthcare practitioners onboard to brainstorm strategies for the person you're caring for may be the most useful approach.

Also, the non-pharmaceutical interventions proposed here are not to minimize the benefits of medical intervention. Instead, these are set out to provide alternative options. It's common to throw pills and medication at issues such as dementia, but this is not always what someone may need to live a thriving and satisfying life after the diagnosis. Please confer with your doctors to identify what the best approach to treating your loved one would be. In some cases, a combination of non-pharmaceutical approaches and medical intervention may be necessary depending on the stage of dementia as well as the person being treated.

Dealing With Memory Loss and Confusion

Forgetfulness is a common experience for people with dementia. Memory loss and confusion may make it hard to hold conversations and focus even in the early stages of dementia. Memory issues can affect people in multiple ways; some may struggle to retrieve old information while others could find it hard to create new memories. The main cause of memory loss in dementia is damage to the brain.

Managing Memory Loss and Confusion

It's important to try different options when it comes to managing dementia-related issues to figure out what the best approach is for your loved one. Some options include:

- Build on strengths

  - If someone has always been a great planner, let them plan stuff throughout the day.

  - Nurturing a person's strengths can stimulate cognitive functioning and help manage memory issues in various areas.

- Encourage time management

  - Set fun tasks with timers on when to finish them; this will help keep the mind active and occupied.

  - Give the person something to do every day at a certain time because routines promote concentration and timeliness.

- Take each day as it comes

  - Some days will be better than others; don't panic when some days things seem hard to control but give each experience the attention it needs.

- Organization

  - Keep items in places so they can be easily found.

○ It reduces agitation which maintains proper memory function.

Each dementia case is different, so treat everyone you encounter with empathy and compassion for their unique situation.

Sleep Issues and Sundowning

A dementia diagnosis tends to increase confusion and restlessness a bit more during the afternoon into the evening—known as sundowning. Symptoms of dementia tend to worsen around this time, so the person is likely to become more agitated, absent-minded, and suspicious. The ability to remember things accurately or focus is completely limited at night, and the person will likely show impulsive behaviors that can put them at risk. Sundowning is scary, and it gets worse as dementia progresses.

The restlessness experienced at night can result in sleeping problems, too. Some people with dementia may have a better time sleeping during the day and have more difficulty resting at night. It's possible for someone with dementia to also have challenges telling the difference between day and night time. Some people may not be as active as they once were, so they may find that their energy lasts longer and sundowning happens more often. Luckily, sleeping issues are often a stage that passes.

Causes of Sleeplessness and Sundowning

The causes of nighttime action are plenty ranging from medical reasons to environmental factors. Let's take a look at some of the things you can consider when trying to pinpoint what causes your loved one to battle restlessness.

Medical Causes

- Illness

    o Not being medically well is a huge reason for sleep troubles and sundowning. Any physical pain caused by ulcers, diabetes, congestive issues, and so on may be a reason.

- Change in sleeping patterns

    o With age, people could get less sleep than usual.

    o Snoring may disrupt sleep.

    o Sleep apnea can cause issues.

Environmental Causes

- The resting space at night

    o The bedroom may be too hot or cold.

    o Inadequate lighting makes it difficult to rest.

- Changes in the environment

    o Moving homes and being in unfamiliar spaces can trigger symptoms.

    o Disorientation can arise by not recognizing the way around one's home.

Managing Sleeplessness and Sundowning

The medical and environmental causes of sundowning and sleeping issues can be frustrating for both the carer and the person living with dementia. Learning how to manage these behaviors can improve the experience of everyone involved in dementia care.

Managing Medical Causes

- Involve a doctor

  - Only a medical professional can provide viable steps to manage the medical complications that influence dementia behavior.

  - Medical check-ups are a great start to identify and treat the physical symptoms that someone may be experiencing.

- Ask questions

  - What medication can they prescribe for bedtime?

  - Are there any possible side effects of the medication?

  - Can an assessment be conducted on the person with dementia to ensure that they get all the medical interventions they need?

  - Are there any lifestyle recommendations from the doctor that could bring balance to a person at night?

Managing Environmental Issues

- Consistency

  - Keep the space and routines as consistent as possible.

- o A person with dementia needs some sort of normalcy and stability to manage all the things that the condition throws at them.

- Adequate light

  - o Poor lighting can contribute to irritation, depression, and other experiences that can worsen the symptoms of dementia.

  - o Shadows and glares can increase the chances of hallucinations and make it hard to manage sleeplessness and sundowning.

  - o Install night lights to manage confusion and disturbances at night; these could also make the environment easier to see and navigate.

- Comfortability

  - o Ensure that the bed for the person to sleep in is comfortable enough.

  - o If the person refuses to sleep in their bed, choose alternative options such as the sofa or a comfortable mattress.

  - o Put familiar objects in the person's room such as pictures of family and favorite decorative items to help them feel more oriented with their surroundings.

  - o Set a radio on the person's side table to play soft, relaxing music.

- o Keep daytime clothes and items away during the night to establish a clear boundary between night and day.

  - o Gently remind the person when it's time to sleep.

- Exercise and a proper diet

  - o Create an exercise routine for the day. Even if it's a brief walk or two daily, it will help reduce energy and promote better sleep at night.

  - o Limit the consumption of caffeine in products such as coffee, tea, chocolate, and cola during the day; remove them altogether by 5 p.m.

  - o Introduce medically recommended forms of meditation in the afternoon to prepare for the night.

  - o Encourage a light snack before bed to minimize hunger during the night.

  - o Prepare herbal teas and warm milk to stimulate a restful state.

Managing dementia behaviors is not easy, so give yourself credit for how hard you try to express empathy and kindness. Also, if you do fall short at times and your emotions get the best of you, it's always good to apologize to the person you're trying to help. Though dementia may limit some cognitive functions, the people who live with it still have emotions and feelings, so an apology when you do them wrong will go a long way to helping them feel safe. Next, let's explore some of the techniques and strategies that you can use for dementia care.

CHAPTER 3

Providing Compassionate Care– Techniques and Strategies

Those with dementia are still people, and they still have stories, and they still have character, and they're all individuals, and they're all unique. And they just need to be interacted with on a human level.

–Carey Mulligan

Compassionate care is the practice of providing care to uphold respect, honor, and dignity. According to the National Health Service (NHS) in England (2015), compassionate care is anchored by six essential elements: care, compassion, competence, communication, courage, and commitment. For the purpose of this book, let's build on these components from a lens of compassionate care in dementia. The element of care refers to the caretaker's ability to deliver health support that improves well-being and advocates for people at every stage. Compassion is about establishing relationships between the caretaker and patients which is built on kindness and dignified practices.

Alternatively, competence refers to the capacity that a caretaker must have to understand the patient's personal and social needs. Competence is connected to one's field of expertise, technical knowledge, and awareness that allows them to perform caretaking duties effectively based on research and evidence. As with any successful relationship, communication is integral to the success of compassionate care. Every caretaker's ability to listen nonjudgmentally, remain calm, and be inclusive can help them provide an optimal level of care. Communication is an essential aspect of compassionate care because it benefits both the recipients and the providers of care. Courage, on the other hand, enables caretakers to do the right thing for those in care. It equips caretakers with the ability to speak up when there are concerns, ask questions, and have the vision as well as the tenacity to embrace the obstacles in dementia care.

Lastly, the commitment element of compassionate care is the vow that caretakers make to provide optimal care to improve the experience of those in care. Commitment is all about taking action when it is required by using healthy techniques to meet the needs and overcome the difficulties of dementia care. The main point of this chapter is to provide information on how you can ensure a safe and dementia-friendly environment for those in care. This chapter will also talk about managing daily activities, personal care, ensuring proper nutrition, and handling medical appointments and medications.

Setting Up a Dementia-Friendly Environment

People are commonly the most vulnerable when they need dementia care. How you show up as a caregiver can have an immense influence on the comfort of those in care. Compassionately caring for someone with dementia is about noticing, feeling, and responding to a patient's experience to alleviate suffering. Recognizing what someone needs, tolerating the challenges, and staying motivated to meet the requirements for both are massive parts of compassionate care. The environment that a person with dementia is exposed to matters, and it can either promote care or deprive it. In this case, setting up a dementia-friendly environment is an excellent start to promoting compassionate care.

Symptoms of confusion, forgetfulness, and difficulty with recollection can be a roadblock to knowing where things are and how things work in an environment. Setting up a dementia-friendly zone takes these symptoms into account. It's essential to apply any major changes to an environment during the day, so you can help someone with dementia be acquainted with their surroundings. A dementia-friendly environment can help a person live independently for as long as it takes before the condition worsens. Dementia-friendliness also prevents the immediate need for someone to be moved to a healthcare facility so they can enjoy the comfort of their space—at least for the first couple of years after the diagnosis. Consider the following tips to create a dementia-friendly environment in areas such as the kitchen, bedrooms, living areas, bathrooms, gardens, and more.

Lighting

Good lighting helps with visibility. Things are much clearer in a well-lit setting compared to a poorly lit one. Good lighting reduces the chances of tripping and accidental falling. Being in a well-lit environment can help someone find things more easily because the light helps to see clearly. Dementia causes impairments in understanding and visual capacity, therefore, lighting is a vital part of ensuring dementia care.

Tips to Promote Better Lighting in a Dementia-Friendly Setting

- Clean windows to allow the light to come through.

- Move large curtains, decorations, furniture, and plants away from the window to prevent blocking the light.

- Bring in extra lighting such as lamps and brighter bulbs; if it's safe, these will add more light to the environment.

- If it's affordable, include sensor lights that automatically sense motion for situations when the person needs to find their way around at night.

- Incorporate dim switches to allow for a better light adjustment from the day to night.

- Incorporate less harsh light around bedtime.

- Adjust the TV settings to ensure that there's more surrounding light coming through than from the source.

- Consider touch-operated lights and lamps to simplify adjusting for brightness.

Living with dementia can make it hard to notice things; that's why it's important to allow light in through clean windows and other avenues. Darkness and shadows can incite confusion, fear, and frustration; well-lit areas control the aforementioned. An adjustment as simple as daylight coming through the windows can help a patient monitor what time of the day it is so they can be on time for things like dinner, activities, and getting ready for bed. Accommodating dimmer light switches can give the illusion of daylight and help the person control the amount of light needed. This is great for nighttime when light should be lower to promote better sleep. Lighting can also prevent sadness, loneliness, isolation, and other conditions that can be perpetuated by the darkness.

Assistive Technology

Assistive technology is any device or system that supports people who have dementia to cope with daily responsibilities (*Assistive Technology for Dementia*, n.d.). This technology can help with movement, orientation issues, and memory among other things. A range of systems can improve dementia care such as phone apps that remind the person to eat, or music apps that can help soothe frustration. Assistive technology can enhance safety, comfort, and independence as well as monitor individual wellness.

Tips for Assistive Technology

- Use smartphones:
  - Clocks
  - Alarms
  - Calendars
  - Checklists
  - Emergency contacts
- Monitor movements:

- o GPS tracking

- o Alert systems

- Monitor appliances:

  - o Include alarm systems for appliances to know when things go on and off.

  - o Have easy-lock settings for things like stoves.

  - o Use vibrating watches to remind you when it's time for medication.

Assistive technology can help your loved one engage in activities and live a balanced life. These can help schedule days and plan activities to ensure that each day is easy to manage. It's up to the family and the people who require care to determine what assistive technologies will work best. As you know, every case is different and should be approached as such.

Noise levels

Controlling noise levels is important in dementia care. Noise can trigger strong emotions and make it hard for a person to feel calm and confident. It's important to consider how you can control noises to prevent startling and confusing a person.

Tips to Manage Noise

- Include carpets, pillows, and curtains; these absorb background noise.

- Avoid vinyl or laminate flooring because it can create noise.

- Turn additional noises off like radios, TVs, and other devices.

Once the noise levels are controlled, it will help those in care feel more comfortable in their own space.

Declutter Spaces

Memory loss in dementia can make it hard to remember where things are, and cluttered spaces make that worse. Decluttering spaces is essential in dementia care; use labels, containers, cupboards, drawers, and whatever else you can think of to get this done. Decluttered environments make the space more functional for someone experiencing dementia. Transparent containers and cupboards or open shelves can make finding items easier. Someone with dementia needs to know exactly where to go when they need to find things.

Tips to Declutter Spaces

- Label items like cupboards, drawers, and containers.

- You can use pictures or colorful texts to highlight what's inside.

- Keep important things such as wallets, keys, and glasses in the same general area.

- Use clear boxes and containers for storage.

- Place important documents in one transparent folder for easy access in emergencies.

- Leave doors open to reduce the risk of getting stuck or closed in.

Decluttered spaces inspire peace of mind and clarity which will be beneficial for people with dementia. Next, the flooring in the space is important and should also be prioritized.

Flooring

Put safety first in every area; flooring should be void of risks that can cause accidental tripping or falling. Uneven floors, rugs, or decorative covers can be a high risk for people with dementia. Focus on keeping things even and smoothed out to allow for balance. Also, avoid dark colors or major theme changes from room to room because that can all be confusing too. Since dementia can also influence how a person sees things, it would be good to avoid shiny floors. Anything shiny may give the illusion of wetness and being slippery. Some patients with dementia will walk more confidently when floors feel even and safe. The colors on the floors and walls should have a contrasting effect to help guide the path for those in care.

Tips for Flooring

- Remove high-risk items:
    - Floor mats, rugs, uneven surfaces, and shiny floors can cause falling and tripping hazards.
    - Tuck away any cables and appliances that pose a risk.
- Be practical:
    - Ensure edges of carpets are held down and are similar colors to the floor.
    - Include colored tape to mark out edges on stairways.

Furniture

Dementia can cause confusion and make it challenging to get around environments. Colors, soft patterns, and lights can make a huge difference in how easily someone with dementia can navigate around. Furniture and finishes that have bright and contrasting colors can help the space stand out and be easy to navigate.

Tips for Furniture

- Avoid backless, armless and low chairs:

  - Chairs with arm rests are great additions because they are easier to stand up from than others.

- Make sure furniture is positioned well:

  - Side tables, rugs, and other items need to be set up in a way that doesn't obstruct the area.

  - Incorporate guiding items such as a pot plant closer to the garden area to help lead the person to the outdoor space.

- Remove items that create confusion:

  - Pictures and mirrors may start to cause confusion; it would be best to remove or cover them, or replace them with familiar items that are less distracting.

  - Use solid-colored furnishings and bedding that complement the walls and floors of the space; this will limit distraction and confusion.

- Keep the setup the same:

  o Moving things around will make it hard for the space to feel comfortable for the person, so keep the setup the same.

  o Don't move things around frequently to prevent accidents.

Brightening the beds, tables, chairs, cloths, walls, and floors, thus, making them noticeable is a great start. Furniture with solid colors is more soothing and approachable compared to stripes and intense patterns which can increase confusion as well as disorientation. It's important to simplify the decoration but still maintain it noticeable enough to stand out. As dementia progresses, it may be beneficial to start removing patterns, paintings, artwork, and mirrors altogether. The more simple the layout, the better it is for the person in care. Of course, when you make changes it's essential to keep things as familiar as possible. For example, keeping the environment's layout the same will help because it's easy to move around when an area is familiar. Next, let's look at how you can help the person in care manage daily activities and self-care.

Managing Daily Activities and Personal Care

Implementing a daily routine filled with important and fun activities is beneficial for the caregiver and those in care. A scheduled day means you spend less time figuring out what to do, and more time just carrying out the day in positive spirits. Managing daily activities requires you to think about the following points:

- What are the person's likes and dislikes?

- What needs to happen even if it's not fun?

- When should a person's medicine be taken?

- What time of day is the person most energetic?

- When is the most optimal bathing time?

- Is the person fit enough to take walks?

    o   Are these better in the early or late afternoon?

Thinking about how to make a simple plan for the day can prevent a lot of complications. Being prepared with a routine can also boost self-care and provide opportunities for intentional personal time to be set aside. Here's a checklist of self-care considerations that should be included in the routine:

- Household chores

- Mealtimes

- Creative activities

    o   Music

    o   Arts and crafts

- Spontaneity

    o   Visiting family and friends

    o   Allowing visitors over

- Intellectual activities

    o   Reading

        ■   Books

- Magazines
  - Games
    - Sudoku
    - Word games
    - Puzzles
- Physical care
  - Light exercise
  - Pampering
- Mental care
  - Journaling
  - Drawing
  - Socializing
  - Meditating

If at any point someone seems bored or uninterested, it may be time to introduce newer activities. Keeping active and managing daily activities is essential to health maintenance in dementia.

Ensuring Proper Nutrition and Hydration

Food and drinks are also essential determinants of health, especially for people with dementia. However, it's common for patients to have lower appetites, lose interest in meals, and not want to eat at set mealtimes. It may also be challenging for dementia patients to notice foods that are the same color as the plate, or to see a plate if the color is similar to the tablecloth. Luckily, despite these roadblocks, there are plenty of ways to ensure proper food intake, nutrition, and hydration in a person with dementia; here are some tips.

Kitchen Settings

Ensure that the items meant for daily use are visible and clearly labeled in an area where they can be easily accessible. The kitchen setting shouldn't make it hard for a patient to reach for essential goods when they need to. Place cereals in plain sight, and mark tea cups and cutlery as required. Be sure to use brightly colored cloths and towels to create contrast between appliances and kitchen surfaces. For example, the kettle and tableware should be different from the plates. Food colors also need to be vibrant and different from the accompanying plates and crockery.

Moreover, clear the kitchen of any clutter. Messiness makes it hard to be productive and consistent so it's important to ensure that the kitchen area stays clean and inviting at all times. A clean kitchen area is more likely to encourage eagerness during mealtimes than an untidy one. In the spirit of tidiness and accessibility, make sure to store food in clear containers to increase visibility. Knowing what's inside a container before opening it makes things much easier for someone with dementia.

Kitchen labels also go a long way in encouraging an appetite. Use a marker or sticky labels to record the dates when the food was placed in the fridge so the person knows when things are still good to eat. Labels clarify any time- and expiration date-related issues regarding food.

Set Reminders

It's also great to set alarms for meal and hydration times throughout the day to prevent dehydration and nutrition deficits. Forgetfulness can make it hard to remember whether a person has eaten or not, so as the caregiver, it's important to stay on schedule and assess the possibilities. You can even place pre-cooked meals and snacks at the patient's disposal daily. To promote hydration, you can buy coasters to brighten up the glasses' positions on the tables in the home which also serve as visual reminders to drink something.

Consistency

Keep the design of the food areas and the rest of the house as familiar as possible. Familiarity increases comfort and reduces confusion. For example, if a kettle breaks, replace the old one with the same model to prevent frustration. Keeping the models the same supports the existing knowledge and memory of the patient regarding how the appliance should be used. This will make it easier for them to prepare drinks that they enjoy without having to learn how to use new appliances from scratch.

Nutritional Value and Advice

Eating nutritious meals is important to keep the body and mind nourished. Good health and strength depend on a good diet, especially for someone with dementia. Having a poor eating plan can increase symptoms of dementia making it even more challenging for the person experiencing it. Basic nutrition matters and the following tips should help you ensure that the person in your care is well-fed and cared for.

Balance the Diet

A good balance of veggies, fruits, whole grains, lean protein, and low-fat dairy products can make for a balanced diet for someone with dementia. For example, great fruit options for dementia include berries and apples. According to Heerema (n.d.), berry options include strawberries, blueberries, and acai fruit which all serve to improve cognitive functioning. Also, studies confirm that apples can assist with memory loss issues. The nutrients from apples can protect the brain from the protein buildup responsible for multiple types of dementia such as Alzheimer's and Lewy body dementia.

Avoid High Cholesterol and Saturated Fatty Foods

Fat is essential for good health, but not all options are good. Heavier fats such as fatty cuts of meat, lard, or butter are a no-go zone. Instead, incorporate fats such as olive oil and lean proteins into the person's diet. Unhealthy fats can clog heart vessels and lead to dangerous health conditions.

Limit Refined Sugar

Almost everything you consume has sugar in it; even fruits have a good amount of natural sugars. Hence, there is no need to add refined sugar to a diet. For example, adding too much sugar to tea makes it unhealthy. Rather, limit refined sugars and try to have most things in their healthy state. Refined sugar is high in calories but low in nutrients, vitamins, fiber, and minerals. You can consider replacing refined sugar with healthier options such as fruit or natural sweeteners.

Reduce Sodium Intake

Adding less salt to a diet can help maintain a healthy blood pressure. Reducing sodium can protect the person you're caring for from experiencing dehydration and multiple health-related issues. If you need to cook with salt, always add just a pinch and nothing more. Healthier alternatives to sodium can include some natural herbs and spices.

Appetite and eating habits may change as dementia progresses, so keep an eye out for the dietary patterns as time goes on. Remember to ensure that the person stays hydrated with small cups of water or healthy liquids throughout the day because that will control hunger and other diet-related things. Now, let's assess how to approach handling medical appointments and taking medications.

Handling Medical Appointments and Medications

Getting someone with dementia to see a doctor can be one of the major challenges in administering care. Medical rooms can be busy and confusing for dementia patients. It can be difficult to understand why these are needed, thus, a loved one can end up fighting with you in an attempt to avoid going. Some tips to help you handle medical appointments and medications better include:

- **Transparency:** Explaining beforehand why the appointment and medications matter can help a patient be more willing to engage. Transparency reduces fear and shows the person that things are being done for their health and benefit, so they become more likely not to fight.

- **Prepare:** Write an email to the doctor with a list of concerns before you take the person in question to the appointment. When the practitioner is prepared with valuable information about the condition and what to expect, they can make an informed decision about how long the session needs to be and what it will include.

- **Book long appointments:** you'll find that people with dementia need longer sessions with the doctor, consequently, they shouldn't be rushed. To be safe, you can book longer sessions to give the practitioner enough time to assess the condition without rushing the patient.

- **Set medication schedules:** Depending on what medicines are prescribed, it could be helpful to organize drugs in schedules and place each into a clear container. Dementia patients need to know that they are being cared for, not cheated or manipulated. So, being transparent about the medications and why they need to take them is key. Schedules not only ensure that you don't forget when it's time for them to take medications but also they also help the patient know what to expect.

Compassionate care is all about being thoughtful and kind to the person you're caring for. At no point should they be forced or yelled at to do anything. Instead, exercise patience and compassion toward them as they navigate the new norm. This brings us to the next point which is compassionate communication in dementia care; related information is in the following chapter.

CHAPTER 4

Communicating With Compassion–Understanding Verbal and Nonverbal Cues

---

To care for those who once cared for us is one of the highest honors.

–Tia Walker

Dementia causes a person's communication to gradually diminish. Something that used to come naturally, suddenly starts to feel overwhelming and stressful over time. It's important to remember that as much as it can get frustrating to communicate with someone who has dementia, it's equally or even more troubling for them to express themselves. Hence, communication in dementia requires patience, understanding, and active listening to get the most out of every interaction.

Verbal and nonverbal communication shows someone how much or little you care. It's important to be mindful and intentional about how you interpret cues from someone with dementia so you can respond to them compassionately. Dementia can create issues with communication as it progresses, therefore, it can be useful to learn what you can look out for and how you can manage it in the future. The main point of this chapter is to help you navigate language barriers in dementia patients, understand and respond to non-verbal cues, as well as use your body language effectively. When communicating, the objective is to create and maintain a connection through active listening, which is another topic discussed in this chapter.

Communicating With Dementia Patients

Changes in communication style are expected in dementia. As a person's cognitive ability worsens, so will their ability to communicate themselves. Communication changes differ from person to person, and these changes are also influenced by the stage of dementia that someone is experiencing. Changes in communication will be more manageable in the early stages compared to later. As dementia progresses, you can expect to see multiple changes in how someone communicates. For example, people with dementia may start to show difficulties in speech, word allocation, vocabulary, and much more. The negative ailments in communication may lead to a person speaking less and less over time. You may even start to experience that some patients are more comfortable communicating themselves through gestures rather than words.

Dementia progression means that communication will also strain with each stage of the condition. So someone who may have had no issues with speech before might gradually find it difficult to use the correct words when trying to describe something or make a point. You may even start to notice the patient losing their train of thought more often than usual. Battling to name familiar items is another sign of communication in dementia. For example, someone may resort to explaining what a pen is in an attempt to get you to pass it to them instead of saying the word itself. A lot of communication changes can be accredited to memory loss and delayed cognitive functioning that causes difficulty in putting thoughts, ideas, and language together.

Communication in The Early Stage of Dementia

Let's start by unpacking what you can expect in the first stage of dementia. Communication in the early stage is typically categorized as mild because few noticeable changes happen. A person with early dementia can interact in meaningful conversations and participate with people in social settings. Situations that require communication are less likely to intimidate someone in the early stage compared to someone experiencing a later stage. Symptoms of communication changes in the early stage of dementia can include

- Repeating words, sentences, and stories

- Battling to find the correct word for something

- Feeling overwhelmed or stressed by overstimulation

It's not easy to accept when your own words fail you, especially when it's due to a condition like dementia. Whenever you start to notice someone struggling with communication at this stage, be kind and patient with them. Also, don't interrupt or rush them to a point unless they ask for help.

Communication in the Middle Stage of Dementia

As dementia progresses, so do communication challenges. In the middle stage of dementia, communication issues also move to a moderate level. The middle stage of communication is generally the longest period for people with dementia, and it can last for a few years before it progresses. When the condition worsens, you'll notice the person has more trouble communicating, and they may need more help and understanding along the way. Symptoms of difficulty communicating at this stage can include:

- Losing one's train of thought

- Using and relying on nonverbal responses to verbal queries

- Struggling to find the right words

- Repeating certain questions

In the middle stage of dementia, people may also find it hard to understand what the speaker is communicating. You may start to notice way more confusion in the patient's eyes and expressions compared to the earlier stage. Ultimately, the middle stage includes the primary speech difficulty and confusion symptoms but worse.

Communication in The Late Stage of Dementia

Lastly, the late stage of dementia is probably the most challenging because at this point communication is immensely strained. Here, a patient with dementia is known to experience severe symptoms and troubles that may last several weeks to years. As dementia progresses, the patient might find difficulty in expressing themselves both verbally and nonverbally. However, they might start to rely on what they can convey using body language such as facial expressions, gestures, and vocal sounds. A person at this stage requires 24-hour monitoring and care.

Hope is not lost at any stage of dementia though, as you can still find effective ways to communicate at the person's level. Next, we explore how you can approach communication at the different stages in a way that helps keep a positive atmosphere between you and the patient. Firstly, above all else, remember to lead all communication with compassion. Caregiving is incomplete without kindness and graciousness, especially toward someone who is struggling with dementia. So if you are going to start anywhere, kindness is the place to begin.

How to Approach Communication With People Living With Dementia

With each stage of dementia, there are also multiple ways that you can approach communication. Starting from the early stage through to the late stage, here's how you can communicate with someone who has dementia.

Approaching Communication In The Early Stage

It's essential to take your cues on how to help the patient you are treating. Don't conclude that someone is struggling with communication issues purely based on the fact that they have been diagnosed with dementia. The diagnosis affects each person differently at every stage, so the troubles that one person may have in the early stage might not resemble those of someone else. Also, just because someone has a dementia diagnosis doesn't always mean they'll show symptoms early; some may experience communication troubles later in progression. It's important to keep including people in conversations—especially the patients themselves—so everyone is treated fairly.

At the early stage, it's beneficial to speak directly to the patient about decisions and things that you want to know rather than going around them to other caregivers or friends. Take the time to actively listen to what a patient needs by paying attention to the message being communicated—verbally and nonverbally. Listen to what the person is thinking, feeling, and wanting from you at the moment, and communicate how you can show up for them. Being direct and upfront during this stage, and every stage to follow is a crucial part of communication. Some communication pitfalls that you can avoid include:

- Interrupting the person when they speak

- Dismissing the person's feelings and experiences

- Getting impatient with the person

- Pulling away or getting distracted

These pitfalls can make it harder to carry out a healthy conversation with the patient and need to be avoided. If you ask a question, be patient enough to hear the answer, and process it so you can truly understand what's being communicated. Later, we'll explore some techniques for active listening that you can use to help you with this point. Also, you don't need to be uptight in a conversation with someone who has the diagnosis. It's okay to keep things lighthearted and laugh along with them if the moment calls for it. What's important is to treat the person as normally as possible so the interactions feel safe and familiar to them. Shared humor tends to lighten up the mood during conversations which makes communicating feelings and messages easier. No matter what, stay engaged, friendly, and supportive of the person you are talking to at all times.

Approaching Communication in the Middle Stage

Of course, in the middle stage of dementia things start to change a bit. At this stage, someone with dementia may need minimal distractions to be able to hold a conversation. Prioritizing one-on-one communication in the middle stage of dementia is important. You can prioritize one-on-one conversations by following the next steps.

Speak In A Quiet Environment

Given how easily distracted someone in the middle stage of dementia may be, it's essential to speak where communication can happen uninterrupted. External factors can easily become a distraction when spaces are noisy and loud. It would be great if you can start by ensuring the space is calm before talking. Also, a quiet space can encourage relaxation which allows for the person to feel at ease with you during the conversation.

Communicate Slowly

Another thing is speaking slowly. Gradual communication gives the person time to process the message without feeling rushed or panicked to understand what's being communicated. Communicating slowly also helps with clarity in a conversation. When you express yourself, it helps the next person understand what you're trying to convey. Speaking in an unhurried manner limits confusion in a conversation and it helps each person play their part. For example, you know what the person needs at the moment and can cater to them accordingly. Also, the patient gets to know what protocols to follow to assist their journey with dementia. You can communicate slowly by:

- Giving the person plenty of time to respond so he or she can think about what to say

- Remaining patient and offering reassurance

  o Try by saying, "You are doing a great job" and, "I'll stay here with you until you feel better."

- Asking closed-ended questions to prompt "yes" or "no" answers

  o For example, "Would you like some coffee?" instead of, "What would you like to drink?"

- Not criticizing, arguing, offering correction, or belittling

- Paraphrasing what was said for clarity

  o For example, "So you feel sad because the biscuits are finished, is that right?"

- Using visual guidance

  o Images

  o Sticky notes

  o Drawings

Always attempt to understand and find out what the person is trying to communicate. To communicate effectively with someone in the middle stage of dementia you need to lead with kindness and thoughtfulness. You can't be impatient and unconcerned. For instance, if the patient says something you don't agree with, the kindest thing you can do is let it be. There's no need to argue with someone who has dementia because it will only cause more frustration. Instead, be clear about what is expected and offer instructions that the person can follow to prevent getting into a cycle of misunderstanding and arguing. Written notes can also help approach communication during the middle stage of dementia. As forgetfulness increases, it could be useful to have written or visual reminders of things to help the conversation when words start to get overwhelming for the patient.

Maintain Eye Contact

Looking at a person during a conversation helps them know that you are engaged. Eye contact shows interest in what's being communicated, and in turn helps the other person feel cared for and seen. Maintaining eye contact may also help the patient feel safe enough with you to share his or her thoughts.

Communication in the middle stage of dementia lays the foundation for what's coming. At the later stage of dementia, you need to apply the principles you've learned from the first two stages but do so more intentionally and delicately.

Approaching Communication in the Late Stage

Communication with a patient at the latest stage of dementia needs you to be extra careful, kind, and patient. Start by keeping this rule in mind: Always approach a patient from the front and say who you are (*Communicating With People Living With Dementia*, n.d.). Identifying yourself reassures the person that you are approaching with good intentions, and it prevents startling them in the process.

It may be harder for someone with dementia to communicate with words during this stage, so don't shy away from encouraging someone to point to something that can help you understand them better. Even encouraging gestures and the use of nonverbal cues is valuable at this stage.

At every stage of dementia, it's important to treat the person with dignity, compassion, and respect. It's okay if sometimes you don't know how to respond to the communication; your mere presence can be calming and familiar to someone battling cognitive changes caused by dementia.

Understanding and Responding to Nonverbal Cues

Body language of nonverbal cues is a way of communicating that doesn't involve speaking. For example, people can communicate with facial expressions, physical gestures, and sounds. Dementia patients tend to lose the ability to emote through speech, so nonverbal cues become the comfortable standard for communication. Some nonverbal behaviors are easily noticeable such as aggression, harsh tone, and losing interest in once enjoyable activities. However, other nonverbal cues can be subtle.

Typically, dementia patients communicate nonverbally to express how they feel, when words fail to do the job. Body language in dementia patients can sometimes appear intentional, but it's not. Though responding to the behavior can be challenging, it's important to remember that the person who has dementia is also having trouble getting you to understand them. Nonverbal cues that seem abrasive or aggressive can signal distress; perhaps the patient's needs aren't being met successfully. Your position as the caregiver is to keep calm and do your best to understand the behavior.

If you pay attention, a person's body cues can guide you about how they feel and what they might be trying to express. Be open to assessing the person's posture, as slouching or turning into themselves can signal fear or discomfort. Then, work to understand what the cause of this could be. Also, take note of their facial expressions because those can help you identify when a person feels sad, frustrated, happy, or confused. Paying attention to simple nonverbal expressions can help you use a process of elimination to identify, understand, and respond to dementia behaviors.

Nonverbal communication can vary from person to person. Understanding how someone communicates nonverbally can help you respond to them promptly, and more efficiently. To start understanding how someone behaves, you need to study their behavioral patterns. It's always helpful to know what someone's normal patterns of behavior are so you can recognize the changes as they happen. Keeping a journal to notice these behaviors can also help you understand and address them more appropriately. Jot down what you notice in terms of expressions and body language so you can care for the person appropriately.

Why Someone Uses Nonverbal Communication

People communicate through body language, touch, and gestures the majority of the time whether they have dementia or not. Only 45% of human communication is verbal, while the majority reflects nonverbal cues (*Behavior in Dementia as a Form of*

Communication, 2020). Most nonverbal cues are natural behaviors that expose what we are thinking and feeling, and this tends to follow a pattern. Every person has a particular response to being happy as they do when frustrated or upset.

Many nonverbal behaviors are triggered by certain changes and experiences, and it's crucial to keep that in mind when working to resolve tensions with a patient who has dementia. The person could be reacting a certain way based on something you said, did, or a sudden change in the atmosphere. For example, a large bang can startle someone resulting in the nonverbal response of fright.

Tips for Nonverbal Communication With Someone Who Has Dementia

Leading with empathy is the most important way to effectively communicate with someone who has dementia. When you put yourself in someone else's shoes, you become less prone to judging them harshly. Empathy requires you to imagine how it must feel to be misunderstood because of your diagnosis. It also requires you to look within for the type of compassion that acknowledges the challenge of experiencing memory loss, difficulty with self-expression, and battling with what is supposed to be familiar to you. When you approach the nonverbal cues from a dementia patient from this lens, you are far more likely to respond appropriately.

Nonverbal communication possibly demands even more patience than verbal communication because you need to "read" the person next to you to understand them. The patience will come when you work to accommodate the person's nonverbal cues instead of trying to control or change them. Most importantly, don't personalize troubling behaviors because they aren't personally directed toward you. How someone with dementia behaves—much like anyone else in the world—is a result of internal thoughts and emotions. So, keep a sense of humor and flexibility when it comes to addressing certain challenges as far as nonverbal cues go.

Addressing Repetitive Nonverbal Communication

Repetitive behaviors are common in dementia. Often, the patient may not have the words to verbally explain the reasons behind such behavior, hence, knowing what to expect and how to address it could be useful. For example, a person may fold and refold clothes to pack in a bag without any verbal communication. If the patient used to travel during certain impactful times of their life, this repetition may be slightly connected to that memory. Therefore, their frustration of no longer being able to travel may appear through the folding and refolding of clothes.

Instead of arguing with the patient about this behavior, try to turn it into something enjoyable. Perhaps invite the patient to help you fold laundry around that time. Encouraging someone to participate in an activity that distracts them from what they no longer have can reduce frustration and allow them to focus their energy on something valuable. A patient who is given room to interact will feel like they are contributing to their own lives and less like they are losing control. As such, issues like boredom and being upset can be managed. Part of responding to repetitive cues is to find ways to embrace them, rather than force change. It's more helpful to incorporate someone's new norm into the daily schedule than it is to attempt to rock the boat.

Addressing Frantic Nonverbal Communication

Restlessness or frantic behaviors such as pacing around a spot or hostile body language need just as much patience as any other behavior. Primarily, addressing nonverbal cues that seem frantic is about connecting the dots by attempting to understand the source of this behavior. For example, if someone is constantly fidgeting with their clothes, it may suggest that they are uncomfortable and need to be somewhere different. However, instead of assuming the cause for the behavior, it's always great to ask the person if they need help. Checking in with patients gives them a platform to nod "yes" or respond alternatively to the question. Always give the person an opportunity to advocate for themselves—gestures and nonverbal communication included.

Using Your Body Language Effectively

You may not be able to control the symptoms of dementia and how these affect a patient's behavior, but you can be intentional about how you respond. Someone with dementia is also reading nonverbal cues to try and interpret what you are communicating. So, it's equally as important for you to pay careful attention to how you carry yourself. You never want to respond in a disheartening manner to anyone, particularly someone battling changes due to dementia.

Your tone of voice, facial expressions, and how you use your body can convey how you feel in a situation. It's important to check your emotions and care for yourself so you can display kind nonverbal expressions to your loved ones. Ensure that positive body language and gestures match your emotions at any given moment. For example, it's okay to smile during a pleasant situation. Even when you aren't having the best day, ensure that you maintain a friendly, professional, and transparent demeanor so the patient is not negatively impacted by your mood.

If you are battling with your emotional burdens and you start noticing it affects how you interact with people in care, please organize a support system. You can join a group of dementia caregivers in your area to share with people who have similar experiences about the hardships that you encounter. You must prioritize your mental and emotional health so you can be a better caregiver. Talk about the ups and downs as well as the joys and sorrows of dementia care. Better yet, schedule therapy appointments to help you debrief as often as you need to so you can continue to show up to the best of your ability. Taking care of yourself and using your body language effectively is vital to strengthening the connection between you and the patient.

Maintaining Connection Through Active Listening

Active listening is an approach to communication whereby you pay complete attention to both verbal and nonverbal cues when someone has something to share. This is a valuable social skill and interpersonal tool to help you build trust, grow empathy, and maintain strong connections. Active listening skills include:

- Maintaining eye contact during a conversation or when the person you're caring for needs your attention

- Not interrupting the person in care while they speak or attempting to regain their train of thought

- Minimizing distractions to offer your full focus in a situation that requires communication

- Repeating yourself as often as needed for the person in care to grasp what you're saying, and visa versa

- Listening more than you speak

Anyone living with dementia can recognize the efforts that caregivers put in to understand them (Alsawy et al., 2020). Active listening is part of the person-centered approach to caretaking that allows each person's personality and needs to shine through without judgment or force.

Now that you've navigated some communication tips and tricks, let's work on addressing financial concerns when it comes to dementia care. Finances can be an elephant in the room when dealing with dementia, and the next chapter aims to help you navigate this territory.

CHAPTER 5

Navigating the Financial Landscape of Dementia Care

Caregiving often calls us to lean into love we didn't know possible.

–Tia Walker

According to the Alzheimer's Association, the number of Americans who provide dementia care to loved ones is continuously increasing (Samuels, 2023). As it stands, more than 11 million people are caretakers for someone with some form of dementia. Caring for this condition has a relatively massive financial and emotional cost. More than $345 billion was spent on dementia care in 2023 alone—estimated to increase and reach trillions by the year 2050 (Alzheimer's Disease Facts and Figures, n.d.). Some expenses that can be incurred include getting professional help, health care, home modifications, and covering medical demands. Whether you choose in-home care or a private facility, there will be expenses to be paid.

Learning about the financial responsibility behind dementia care can help you prepare for the future. Talking and thinking about finances can be stressful, but it's important to have those conversations so you aren't in the dark about financial expectations. The financial demands of dementia care can be influenced by multiple factors. For instance, the stage of dementia that your loved one is experiencing will determine how much is spent on their care. Things like training a caregiver to administer care if you can't, living rates, and the area you live in can also influence finances.

In this chapter, we navigate the financial challenges and demands that come from dementia care. The chapter also explores information about the costs of dementia care, insurance coverage for dementia patients, the importance of long-term planning, and the value of preparing legal documents ahead of time. Dementia is not something most people can prepare for, but you can gather resources to prevent monetary blindside in this area. Financial information can help reduce the pressure of the upcoming burdens, and keep you at ease knowing that the person you care for is taken care of in this area. Let's explore the potential cost of care and how you can go about planning for cover.

Understanding the Costs of Dementia Care

As dementia progresses and its symptoms intensify, so do the experiences of disorientation, wandering, and mobility issues. When this happens, it increases the possibility of hazardous instances such as falling or getting hurt in some capacity. Hospitalization and the need for medication become more prominent as dementia worsens, therefore, one needs to understand the costs in order to prepare for them.

Medical Costs of Dementia Care

Having a trusted medical team is key to successfully caring for someone with dementia. The first natural step is to get an official doctor's diagnosis so you can know which stage your loved one is in, and how to approach taking care of them. To get a diagnosis, the doctor is likely to provide a baseline assessment of cognitive functioning along with an overall wellness check. This will help you be informed about the progression of your loved one's dementia. Appropriate medical assistance can help someone who is living with dementia manage and sustain a good quality of life.

However, some costs come with medical care for dementia. For example, regularly consulting with a doctor is a medical cost on its own. Also, if your loved one qualifies for treatment, dementia medications and medical care can be expensive. Treating symptoms such as hearing loss and vision impairment, and doing multiple tests to check cognitive progression all require financial backing. Doctors may even suggest certain specialists for some examinations to be conducted which requires more financial involvement. Depending on who you are funded by, some medical insurances can cover areas that include:

- Cognitive assessments and consultations

- Wellness checks

- Dementia care planning

- In-home care (if the doctor prescribed it)

- Up to six months of hospice care at the late stage of dementia

Medical costs tend to feel even worse when you have to pay for everything from your pocket. If the person you are caring for is covered by a medical scheme, care, or aid, then you may be in a better position than someone who is not covered.

Average Monthly Costs of In-Home Dementia Care

Before getting into this, it's important to note that all expenses will be household- and lifestyle-dependent. Nonetheless, the information provided is based on rough estimates that can be used to make general cost determinations. As shared by Samuels (2023), the average cost of in-home care stands at an hourly rate of $30. Of course, rates differ between states, so you may find yourself paying anything from $21 to 50$ per hour depending on where you are.

A huge majority (77%) of elders with dementia prefer to keep some form of independence by staying in their homes after the diagnosis, but symptoms of dementia can complicate things (Samuels, 2023). So in-home care can be useful to help them manage the desire to stay independent while managing dementia. A paid caregiver can keep your loved one engaged, safe, and well-fed during this time. You can have a nurse who assists with daily tasks and general aspects of well-being. For example, hiring someone who can help with cleaning the house, cooking meals, and making sure that the patient takes medication on time. If you use the hourly rate estimations, you could potentially spend up to $2,000 monthly for four to five hours of care each week. Most people don't even make that amount of money in a month, which can be terrifying to consider.

Why In-Home Care For Dementia Is Costly

A lot of training and effort goes into dementia care, so professional caretakers are compensated for the hours of manual work that go into providing compassionate care. Caretaking for someone who has dementia takes extra skill and sometimes additional training which contributes to the expenses. Essentially, a caretaker is paid to not only do their job but to know the patient's needs, symptoms, and uniqueness after being cleared to work at home. Though you may not be able to avoid paying the high fees, you can do your due diligence to ensure that you pick a caretaker who is best suited for your loved one's needs. You are allowed to interview and thoroughly screen caregivers before contracting with them. Keep in mind, the more experience the care provider has, the greater the expense will probably be. Caregivers who are trained to help elderly people with dementia are expected to provide multiple services, some of which include:

- Companionship
  - Social stimulation
  - Conversations
- Assistance with daily living
  - Bathing
  - Cooking
  - Feeding (in extreme cases)
  - Bathing
  - Dressing

- o Cleaning

- Manage symptoms of dementia such as sundowning and forgetfulness

- De-escalation if behaviors become aggressive or reactive

- Reminiscence therapy to minimize anxiety and promote positive thinking

- Encourage at-home activities that promote mental and physical health

- Alleviate care burdens from the family so you can enjoy the time with your loved one

There is obviously so much more that goes into in-home care that's not listed here. It's expensive, but oftentimes you will find that it's worth budgeting and paying for. In-home care allows you to keep your life normal while you can enjoy the moments you have with your loved ones. Letting someone else manage the pressure allows you to focus on immediate responsibilities, and also maintain a healthy family dynamic between yourself and the relative in care. In-home care is not the only cost you'd need to consider for dementia care. Next, let's take a look at the others.

Additional and Hidden Costs of Dementia Care

Other costs beyond monetary ones are equally as important to be mindful of. Dementia care is extensive, and it can change your experience of life immensely. Knowing what the hidden costs of dementia are can help you put measures into place to prepare yourself for what's coming.

Emotional and Mental Costs of Care

Dementia care is known to have some tough emotional underpinnings. With high levels of anxiety, stress, and depression, caregivers are more vulnerable to mental and emotional issues than non-caregivers. If you are the one in your family who cares for someone with dementia, it can take an emotional toll. The negative emotional cycle is generally tied to the pressure of balancing care and responsibilities outside of dementia care. Stress can lead to caregiver burnout, which is something many people who provide care to dementia patients experience. Symptoms of caregiver burnout can include:

- High irritability

- Impatience

- Emotional indifference

- Lashing out

To cope with the emotional expense of providing care you need to get yourself acquainted with a good group of people who share a similar experience. Allowing yourself to connect with a group of other caregivers can offer a much-needed safe space for you to vent, get comfort, and be reassured. Other people on the same journey can offer helpful advice to help you manage your own. This can also be an opportunity for you all to empathize with one another while remembering that you aren't alone.

Lifestyle and Professional Costs of Care

Caring for anyone can change the structure of your life; dementia care is no different, in fact, the shift is even more pronounced. Your lifestyle and professional paths are likely to be hugely impacted by the decision to provide dementia care. Whether time is taken from productivity or energy for living the life you once knew, dementia care can be costly. Caring for someone with dementia may bring up certain emergencies that affect your professional availability and performance. For example, you may get a call that requires you to jump into your car and head straight home. Dementia care may demand missing some professional responsibilities to take your loved one to a doctor's appointment and spend time with them on the days when in-home caregivers are off. The unpredictable nature of dementia care can make it challenging to keep to a set schedule and maintain balance in your life.

On top of all this, dementia care responsibilities may drain the enjoyment out of you. Suddenly, you could find it draining to show up for anything in life that requires effort and time. For example, going to work functions or attending social events may be too much for you to give your time, money, and energy to when you are so focused on what's happening at home. While it can be rewarding to know that you are providing indirect or direct care for someone you love, it can also be extremely tiring to keep showing up.

Your feelings and emotions toward the whole experience are valid. However, don't stop being patient and compassionate with yourself. As much as you give kindness to the person living with dementia, you also need to be gracious toward yourself in the process. Dementia care is not easy for anyone, and you need to extend that compassion to yourself, especially on the hardest days.

Exploring Insurance and Other Care Options

Since you are aware of the financial responsibilities of dementia care, it could be useful to explore some Medicare and insurance options to ensure your loved one is covered.

Insurance Options

Different options will cover different needs, so it's good to evaluate what your loved one could benefit from and choose your insurance based on the findings. Luckily, there are a range of insurance options to choose from so you have the luxury of variety.

Option One: Employer-Issued Insurance

Some employers cover the medical expenses that are needed for the person who works for them. However, you need to be aware of the inner workings and expectations of this coverage. Also, this may not be as sustainable of an option compared to the other ones because it covers employees, but what happens when dementia makes it hard to continue work responsibilities? This is something that you must keep in mind moving forward.

Option Two: Long-Term Insurance

When considering the best coverage for your loved one, you need to look out for the stipulations from each policy. Though some insurances may claim to offer solutions for dementia care, there may be some conditions in there that you won't always agree with. Also, it's crucial to note that it's difficult to get insurance for long-term care once someone has already been diagnosed with dementia. Companies may consider late coverage as a liability, so avoid jumping in.

However, if the person you are caring for is already qualified for a policy it's helpful to read the fine print to ensure that they get the best from it. Some useful questions that you can ask in your mission to choose long-term insurance include:

- When can the person claim benefits?

- Are all types of dementia covered?

- How long does it take for payment to reflect after a claim has been made?

- What type of dementia care is covered?

- Are any in-home care options available?

- Are there any in-home care costs that can be covered?

- Is there a maximum payout for someone's lifetime?

Asking questions and doing your research thoroughly is important. Preparation hinges on the knowledge you attain before you are faced with the massive responsibility of dementia care.

Option Three: Life Insurance

Certain life insurance policies permit patients to claim their benefits and use them to pay for long-term care options while they are still alive. Of course, every policy will differ from the next.

Option Four: Medigap Insurance

Medigap is a private insurance option that covers copayments, gaps in coverage, and deductibles. It's a worthy consideration if you want to supplement your Medicare or insurance at the moment.

Personal Assets

Any property, investments, and individual savings are referred to as personal assets. Each of these things can be used as a source of income during the period of dementia care. Money brought in from personal assets can cover items, medications, and services that are needed during dementia care.

Employee Benefits

If the person in care chooses to continue work during the early stage of dementia, there could be some employee benefits available for them. For example, paid leave, short-term disability options, and supportive payment plans. It's important to pay close attention to the offers that your employer provides so you can get on top of benefits earlier rather than later.

Government Assistance

In addition to private insurance and care options, a patient could benefit from government assistance. Public programs are readily available to people who are living with dementia, and these can provide income support or dementia care services to individuals who need it. Some examples include supplemental security income (SSI), social security disability income (SSDI), and more.

Retirement Benefits

The payouts and benefits from retirement plans can be a serious financial resource for people living with dementia. Benefits can be useful even before the retirement age rolls by. For example, individual retirement accounts (IRAs) and annuities can be fundamental to set up as financial nets that can help in the future. The earlier you have a plan in place, the better it will be.

Someone living with dementia has the option to withdraw money from their IRA or any employee-funded plan even before the age of 59 (Paying for Care, n.d.). However, your loved one would need to pay some form of tax towards this withdrawal. It's great to research the specific agreement that you've signed.

Community Support Services

Multiple communities offer affordable and sometimes free support services that include transportation, meal deliveries, support groups, and other valuable services. It's essential to lean on the community during this time. You can even include informal care arrangements with family and your trusted circle of people.

Planning for Long-Term Care

As dementia progresses, planning for long-term care becomes more essential. Once the symptoms of dementia are in high gear it gets hard to navigate care plans, that's why families and caregivers need to start planning early. If you have no idea where to start, you should include professionals such as geriatric care managers, nurses, and social workers in the process of creating a care plan.

Planning for long-term care can ensure that you have the tools and resources you need to provide care at home and even at external facilities. It might be helpful to start considering the following things as you plan for long-term care:

- What are the proposed living arrangements as dementia progresses?

- How can the person's assets be managed to support their diagnosis, needs, and safety?

- What community services can be useful for the person?

- How much will the cost of living become as you work to cope with the diagnosis?

- What decisions need to take priority?

- How far ahead do strategies need to be put in place to ensure a seamless transition if one needs to happen?

Long-term care needs to openly discuss every area of a person's life that will be affected by their dementia over time. So, the family and advisers need to come together to explore care options, steps that will be taken as dementia progresses, residential care, and an array of other important things.

Residential Care Options

Most people want to stay at home even after being diagnosed with dementia. Living independently with some in-home care is generally an option for people who are in the early stages of dementia, but it can get tricky for people in the later stages. Keeping an open mind to changing living arrangements can be a helpful part of long-term planning. Even if staying at home is the goal, it wouldn't hurt to have backup options. Residential care outside of one's home does not need to be seen as a bad thing, instead, you can choose care settings that fit your family's needs and cater to the person in care.

However, if you believe that there will come a stage when residential care is a viable option, then this information is invaluable. The following considerations should help you decide whether making the change from home to residential care is necessary:

- Is the person in care unsafe in the current setting?

- Does the state of the person's health put them and the caretaker at risk?

- Are the person's needs still being met?

- Is providing in-home caretaking away from other responsibilities?

- Would social interaction, structure, and the community from residential care be beneficial at all?

When discussing residential options with someone who has dementia, it's important to honestly list out the pros and cons of all potential options. Wanting to stay at home is always the first desire, but it may not be what's best in the long term.

Care settings can include a range of environments tailored to varying needs. From retirement housing options to memory care units, there's something for everyone living with dementia.

Retirement Housing

People who can still live independently are more suitable for retirement housing. Symptoms are easier to manage during the early stage of dementia, so people can do with the moderate supervision provided in retirement homes. Retirement housing offers social and interactive opportunities that can boost a patient's mood and help them live a great life.

Memory Care Units

Alternatively, memory care units are created to meet the individual requirements of people living with dementia. These care units typically take up multiple forms including assisted living and secured units. Memory care units will provide services that are specific to the type of care each patient needs. Care units are also accompanied by trained staff and special activities.

Long-Term Care Facilities

In short, long-term care facilities are more hands-on nursing homes. These offer 24-hour care and long-term medical services. Typically, someone at the tail-end of the middle stage or experiencing the late stage of dementia will need this type of care. When deciding on which route to take, it's important to be honest about what stage of dementia your loved one is in.

Supported Care

Also referred to as assisted living, supported care bridges the gap between independence and community housing. It offers patients the chance to maintain personal agency while living with a team of registered nurses and staff who can prepare meals, neaten housing, and offer health services and urgent care. However, not every supported care establishment is tailored to dementia patients so ask before agreeing to move.

Planning Tips and Advice for Alzheimer's Long-Term Care

Preparing for long-term care can feel overwhelming at first. However, you start to feel at ease as the plans are solidified and confirmed by the relevant parties. Follow this checklist as a starting point for your preparations; use it as a guide and be open to changes that may need to happen along the way:

1. Jot down a list of bulleted discussions that you can share with your family when you meet about planning for long-term care.

2. Gather all important documents that will be needed for the person's care, and place these in one area so they can be easy to access in the event of an emergency.

3. Remember to update all documents regularly, and as situations change.

4. You should make and keep copies of important healthcare information or directives in separate medical files.

5. Assign permission and power to a lawyer or medical doctor to communicate to in-home caregivers if needed.

Those are five things that you can do as far as considerations go after the person has been diagnosed. Plans can change as dementia progresses, so be flexible and do everything in the best interest of the person in care. Early planning will reduce stress and confusion in the future.

Legal Considerations and Preparations

As far as planning goes, legal considerations and preparations are equally crucial to successful dementia care. Assessing and deciding the legalities is exceedingly more important for someone with dementia, particularly getting an early start. When the plan is set into motion early, it allows the patient to get involved in the decisions that are made for his or her future. Planning eliminates guessing games and confusion by setting everything out in stone before serious action is required.

Discuss Legal Capacity

A person's legal capacity refers to their ability to comprehend the information presented to them as well as the consequences of behaviors (*Planning Ahead for Legal Matters*, n.d.). For example, if the patient can articulate themselves and understand the meaning of legal documents, then they can sign or agree. Lawyers can inform on the level of legal capacity required for someone to sign certain documents.

Before Signing Legal Documents

It's important to sign documents when legal capacity is clear or professionally confirmed by doctors and lawyers alike. Before someone with dementia signs any legal material it needs to be thoroughly explained. Also, all parties must reach a mutual understanding that the person is aware of what's being asked. Next, seek medical advice particularly if someone's legal capacity is in doubt. Lastly, review existing documentation to make sure that everything is up-to-date.

Talks With a Lawyer

Lawyers are valuable people to consult for legal preparations and advice. For example, these are people who can guide you in steps for legal documents and so on. When dealing with dementia in elderly people, it's good to meet with a lawyer who specializes in elder laws. If you already have an attorney, consult about various legal resources that you may need before moving forward.

Quick tips

Discussion options when you meet with your attorney can include:

- Health care, long-term choices, and making decisions for things related to the residential setting or living situation

- How to manage estate, dementia care, and property

- Coverage for long-term services, medical care benefits, and insurance policies

- Make sure you bring copies of the following:

- List of assets (bank accounts, safe deposit boxes, vehicles, estates, and so on)

- List of beneficiaries, account holders, and owners

- Copies of all property planning documents, estate deeds, income tax returns, life insurance policies, long-term care policies, and other important documents

It would also be great to consult with the lawyer about what you should bring to the meeting so you can show up prepared. Planning for the future can feel overwhelming, but it is rewarding once everything is in place. The next chapter offers a more lighthearted tone as we discuss self-care and balancing personal needs in the dementia care journey.

CHAPTER 6

Self-Care for the Caregiver–Balancing Your Needs

Caregiving has no second agendas or hidden motives. The care is given from love for the joy of giving without expectations, no strings attached.

–Gary Zukav

The emotional cost of caregiving can create havoc in your life, that's why it's important to take care of yourself each step of the way. Whether you are a caregiver or not, self-care is an essential part of mental and physical well-being. Taking care of yourself minimizes stress and puts you in a good mood which improves the way you show up in the lives of others.

Self-care is particularly important in dementia care because it helps you develop compassion and patience for yourself that you can take into caring for patients. Anything that rejuvenates and nurtures your mind, body, and spirit is a form of self-care. Balancing your needs with the responsibilities that come with dementia care will prevent tiredness and resentment. It will also lift your spirits because doing things into which you could channel yourself promotes positive feelings.

As a caregiver, you spend countless hours catering to someone else's needs, and it's easy to forget that you need to meet your own in the process. You can even become so focused on providing care that you push your self-care to the side. Dementia care is challenging work, and the best way to succeed in caring is to make sure that you are your best, most empowered self. This chapter encourages you to prioritize self-care in your life because caring for others requires you to care for yourself too. The chapter explores the importance of self-care and how to maintain overall well-being in dementia care.

The Importance of Self-Care in Caregiving

Think of self-care as a way to reward yourself for the hours of effort and energy you put into caregiving. Self-care is important because caregivers are vulnerable to compassion fatigue, anxiety, and depression due to the selfless nature of providing care services. Taking care of yourself is probably the only time you'll get to ensure that your needs are met as often as you work to meet the needs of people around you. The emotional energy that goes into taking care of patients means you are using up fuel from your tank, and self-care is a way to refill it.

Making sure that you are cared for emotionally, physically, and socially is key to performing at your best. It is also an integral part of preventing burnout and feeling overworked. Caregiving comes with a range of emotions, and self-care is a way to ensure that you feel supported in your journey. Providing care is not straightforward, especially when the caregiver is not prioritizing their well-being. If you believe that you may be neglecting the area of self-care, hopefully understanding its importance will sway you to take it more seriously.

Self-Care Minimizes Stress

Self-care is a great mediator between your responsibilities and stress. Caregiving can feel like mountains are on your shoulders but self-care helps to reduce that pressure. Self-care is known to prevent or reverse symptoms of exhaustion, being overwhelmed, negativity, and feelings of helplessness (Why Self-Care for Caregivers is Important for Their Mental Health, 2017). It helps to improve mental, physical, and emotional health by minimizing the stress that you may feel due to the demands of caregiving.

Self-Care Prevents Mental Health Issues

Lower levels of stress prevent other mental health issues. When you feel overwhelmed and do nothing about it, your risk of emotional instability increases. However, the game changes when you decide to prioritize self-care. Caring for yourself can treat and ease the symptoms of mental health conditions such as depression, chronic stress, and aggression (Why Self-Care for Caregivers is Important for Their Mental Health, 2017). Even caregivers who haven't received mental health diagnoses benefit from self-care practices.

Self-Care Fuels You so You Can Care for Others

Caregivers can't give from an empty cup. Though taking care of yourself may not feel natural, especially as someone who prides themselves in caring for others, self-care is essential. It is a way to fuel you so you can care for others. Self-care enlarges emotional, mental, and physical capacity so you can think clearly and make good choices for yourself. Taking time for your needs will make you feel more at ease so you can replace impatience, tiredness, and irritability with more positive counterparts.

Caregiving can feel overwhelming, and taking breaks to recoup can do wonders for you. It's normal to battle with unique and challenging obstacles as a caregiver, but you need to get into the habit of addressing these with care. Self-care is an opportunity to connect and energize yourself for the sake of your well-being. When you are healthy, so will be your outlook on life. The best part is, self-care is not about being over the top but it's about learning how to balance serving others and doing things that cater to you. Self-care is all about moving, eating well, and building social connections.

Good investments lead to growth. Carving time out of your schedule to care for yourself is an investment into your future, and the next parts of this chapter will explore the multiple ways to practice self-care.

Physical Wellness: Diet, Exercise, and Rest

On average, caregivers provide about 12 hours of care daily and it can take a great emotional, financial, and physical toll (*A Healthy Diet Can Help Caregivers Reduce Stress*, 2020). Your body is what you use to physically accomplish your goals and manage your responsibilities—you can't move without it. In self-care, your physical well-being needs to be one of many priorities. Physical wellness includes taking care of your mind and body through eating healthy, exercising, and resting.

Eat Healthy Food

Caregiving can be so busy that you forget to eat nutritious food. To optimize on time, you may find yourself going for easy-grab meals such as takeaways or processed snacks. However, not eating well can truly impact your health negatively. It can make it even harder for you to provide care and meet your responsibilities. Nutrition is essential for a caregiver because food gives energy that helps you focus on what needs to be done long-term. Working 12-hour days means you need to take care of what you put into your body, especially if you want your energy and good mood to last long.

A healthy diet is a form of self-care that can improve focus, increase energy, and promote productivity. Instead of picking up a quick takeaway of heavily fatty foods, prioritize eating homemade foods with high nutritional value. Eating nutrients such as lean proteins, fruits, veggies, fiber, vitamins, and mineral-rich foods can be a lifesaver; these are things that you should add to your next shopping cart. Also, remember to stay hydrated. Drink water and other healthy drinks such as milk or freshly squeezed, unsweetened juices between meals. Maintaining great hydration can help you manage your hunger and eat moderately.

You should also include healthy snacks between meals such as berries, bananas, or even nuts. A handful of almonds or cashews can be great snack options. Top this off with a great selection of low- or no-fat dairy products such as Greek yogurt and other options. The important thing is to get creative with your food so you feel more excited to dig in during breaks.

Time To Prepare Meals

Meal preparations take time, and sometimes it's time that you may not have at all. If you are fortunate enough to have a housekeeper, then all you need to do is hand over a list of all the foods you'd like made every week. However, if you are like the majority of us who aren't in a position to afford extra help, you may want to pre-plan and prepare your meals.

Depending on your availability, you need to choose two days out of the week to prepare meals beforehand. For example, you can cook food on Sunday to last you through to Wednesday. Then, cook food on Wednesday to cover the following days until Sunday. This will help you have ready meals for most of your week without needing to cook every day. You can also buy containers and label them for lunch and dinner prepared for each of the days ahead. Luckily, you don't need to worry about your food spoiling if you spread your meal prep out regularly. Refrigerators are also great options to use to keep your food fresh throughout the week. So, if you prepare something on Sunday but you intend to eat it the next Wednesday, keep it refrigerated so you can warm it when you are ready to eat it.

Guidelines: A Balanced Diet

To eat balanced, what you eat you need to focus on buying foods that excite you, but are also rich in nutrients. You may need to minimize your intake of certain products just so you can keep in the spirit of good health. The following guidelines can help you excel in the kitchen, here's a list of things you can purchase:

- Apples

- Breadsticks (whole grain or seeded options)

- Broccoli spears

- Carrots

- Cauliflower

- Celery sticks

- Fresh fruits

- Lean protein (fish, chicken, beef, egg, quinoa)

- Nuts (almonds, walnuts, and cashews)

- Green veggies

Remember to:

- Store colorful fruits

- Manage your portions

- Limit sugar, fatty meat, salt, and butter

- Avoid sugary drinks

- Drink loads of water

Your food is covered, but it's not the only part of physical wellness. Taking care of a combination of elements is self-care, so let's explore more.

Exercise

The demands of being a caregiver can make it hard for you to maintain balance in the areas of your life that need it most. Perhaps you used to be an active person who took pride in eating well and caring for yourself, but those things fell to the side once caregiving started. You could be starting to notice yourself sitting more and eating for convenience rather than health.

Signs that you might be neglecting your physical health can include headaches, an imbalance in blood pressure, weight irregularities, and difficulty doing things you used to do with ease. Lack of movement allows the stress you feel from caregiving to settle in your body and make you vulnerable to physical and emotional health conditions. Exercise can help you feel like yourself in the most harsh of circumstances by relieving caregiver stress.

Your well-being is important not only because of the value your work brings but also because your health is your life. The daily goal should be between 30 and 40 minutes of moderate exercise two or three times a week (*Exercising When You're Caring for Someone Else,* n.d.). Ideally, the time you spend exercising per session should be 30 to 40 minutes straight with a few breaks in between.

However, things can get hectic and days can be busy so don't feel pressure if you can't commit to 30 minutes. Other options include breaking that down into 10-minute mini workouts throughout the day, or even committing to at least 25 minutes of intentional walking daily. If the alternative options suit you better, then you can increase the number of times you get active weekly. For example, 25-minute walks can be a weekday thing for you (five days) rather than doing it three times a week. As long as you keep moving, it doesn't always matter how you fit your exercise in.

Also, as you work out, challenge yourself to incorporate cardiovascular exercises into the practice that increase your respiration rate. Breaking a sweat is an opportunity for you to strengthen your lungs. Your breath is an essential part of movement so use it to motivate you to keep going. Physical exercise will increase your energy, strength, and stamina to prepare you for your daily responsibilities. Due to a large number of reasons exercise is beneficial to everyone, especially caregivers.

Exercise Is An Outlet

As previously mentioned, exercise provides relief from stress. You get to channel your energy and effort into something that gets your adrenaline pumping and your blood flowing. Exercise is an outlet for pent-up tension; the release from physical activity helps you clear your mind and find some relaxation. The short time you spend outside or doing something at the gym will improve your mood and your health. This brings us to the next point.

Exercise Is Protection and Prevention

The relief and relaxation that exercise provides minimize the risk of illnesses. For example, physical activity stimulates the release of endorphins that reduce symptoms of stress, fatigue, and depression (*The Benefits of Exercise and Physical Activity for Caregivers and the Individuals Receiving Care*, 2020). Exercise works to reduce hypertension, protect you from heart disease, and prevent lifestyle-induced diabetes.

Exercise is about feeling and looking good as well as staying fit. Committing to physical activity gives your body and mind the chance to refresh. The more energy you can use up during the day through exercise, the better rest you'll get at night.

Rest

The demands of caregiving can be strenuous for the most resilient people, hence, rest is crucial. Getting quality sleep goes hand in hand with a healthy diet and exercise. Rest provides temporary relief for caregivers, it's the only time that your mind and body get to calm down and reset. You are moving and doing things every other time of the day, and the demands of the day can get the best of you without rest.

Many caregivers battle with sleep deprivation because the idea of resting while someone needs your support can be scary. Factors like worry and changes in your routine can contribute to poor sleeping patterns. You may be super concerned about the person you're caring for and that can play in your mind a bit more than you'd like it to. However, it's important to prioritize sleeping at night and breaks during the day.

Figuring out how to unwind from a stressful day takes practice but once you figure it out, it helps you continue to care for yourself and the person in care. It's important to find a time for rest during the day and at night, the following tips can guide you on how.

Take Advantage of Day-Breaks

Taking breaks between tasks during the day is a way to preserve energy. Breaks promote long-term effectiveness, thus, you can perform to the best of your ability. Self-care is all about prioritizing overall wellness, and taking mini-breaks will help with this. Another great option is 15-minute power naps. If it's possible to seclude yourself during the day for just a few minutes, do that, particularly if it poses no risk to the person you're caring for or your career. You can also opt for short intervals of 5-minute meditation to simply close your eyes and tune into yourself. A quick break can be the difference between burnout and feeling refreshed.

Prioritize Sleep: Bedtime Routines and Comfortable Environments

To fall asleep at night you need to prioritize sleep, and you can do this by establishing a bedtime routine for yourself. Bedtime routines help you prepare your heart and mind for sleep. The relaxation that comes from preparing for bed can help prevent nighttime disturbances and improve your quality of sleep.

One option for a bedtime routine is to put your phone and other electronics away at least two hours before bed. Try to listen to white noise as you cuddle into the warmth of your sheets. If any worrying thoughts come to your mind during this moment of silence, then keep a journal beside your bed to write these down and address them the next morning. It's essential to do things that promote calmness before bed because routines and comfort help you fall asleep quicker and better.

Also, make sure that your sleeping environment is comfortable; this is paramount to getting quality rest at night. For example, no matter how tired you are, always sleep on a comfortable bed rather than opting for the couch. Ideally, the bed should be in your room so the rest period is personalized and comfortable for you.

If you are worried about how you'll hear the person in care when you are in a separate room, there are solutions for that. For example, use a baby monitor to give you comfort in the fact that you'll hear it when someone genuinely needs your help during the night. Another way to create a comfortable environment is to sleep in a dark room, so draw the curtains or close the blinds. Soft tones and quietness signal the brain to fall into a state of relaxation. Lastly, eliminate any noises and lights that can distract you from falling asleep.

Investing in your physical well-being will promote emotional wellness, too. Remember, your physical and mental health are connected—the wellness of one impacts that of the other.

Emotional Wellness: Dealing With Feelings of Guilt and Grief

According to information shared by *Exercise for Caregiver Health* (n.d.), caregivers experience huge amounts of emotional and physical strain. The caregiver statistics from the information show that a higher number of women caretakers (35%) experience caregiving stress compared to 25% of men in the same field. Even so, everyone should take care of their emotional and physical health at all times.

The Emotional Side of Caregiving

Caring for someone can stir up a wide range of mixed emotions. Some days you may feel like the work you do is rewarding, while on others you could feel a sense of dread and disconnection. The emotional side of caregiving is normal, but it can be draining if you don't notice how the work affects you. Emotions can surface in different ways from day to day. Plenty of strong emotions are associated with caregiving; a few examples include doubt, frustration, stress, sadness, and guilt. You may feel these at different times and be triggered by various things.

Doubt

As a caregiver, you may constantly doubt your abilities. You might question whether the effort you are putting in is enough, or if there's anything more you can do. However, doubt gets you nowhere further than you are. You need to learn to embrace the moment and permit the process to be what it is. Remember that you are learning, and it is normal to wonder what more you can do. As long as you keep showing up, things will fall in place eventually.

Frustration

Caregiving can bring up feelings of frustration sometimes. You could feel underappreciated or trapped in a situation, especially when crying for dementia patients. Most times you won't get the gratitude that you deserve for the effort you put in, and that can create internal turmoil. Frustration can lead to impatience and losing your temper in moments. When you blurt out something you don't mean or respond irritably to the person in care, it is a huge sign of frustration that needs to be addressed.

If you act out of frustration, the next best step is to forgive yourself. Also, take a break and clear your mind so you can come back and do better. You need to give yourself the pauses you need throughout the day so you can keep a cool, clear head.

Stress

The list of stressors in dementia care is long, you could feel stressed about things that haven't even happened yet. Stress can make you feel out of control, and it can make it hard for you to care with compassion. You might think thoughts like, "What if something goes wrong and I'm not close enough to fix it?" or,

"What if I'm doing this incorrectly?" Stress is often a sign that you need to give yourself grace and tap into self-care habits. As long as you are doing the best you can, it is enough.

Try to avoid overthinking. Instead, plan for the things that you stress about. For example, call someone to step in when you aren't close enough to provide care, or get guidance from doctors and the medical team for the things you aren't sure of.

Sadness

Caregivers can feel a huge wave of sadness when observing the impact that dementia has on patients. When you witness someone not at their best, it can trigger sympathy and sadness within you. However, you need to find healthy ways to cope with sadness. Take a moment to cry if you need to. Adding journaling as a form of release can also help you get your mind around strong emotions. All your feelings are valid given the situation that you are in, so don't be afraid to honor what you feel.

Guilt

Sometimes self-care and honoring your own needs can bring up feelings of unworthiness and guilt. In caregiving, guilt is common because you're constantly feeling bad for choosing to take care of yourself. You can also feel a sense of guilt that you still have the cognitive ability that your patient struggles with. However, go easy on yourself when you feel overcome by guilt. Remind yourself that you are involved where you can be and your input makes a difference.

Ways to Ease Caregiver Guilt

Your emotional capacity needs you to work on reducing the intensity of your feelings, and using the self-care tricks mentioned earlier is a great place to start. Caregiver guilt is far more common than people recognize. You could feel guilty for the little frustrations you show throughout the process. Guild can stem from feeling resenting the person in care for the amount of energy and effort it takes to support them. Sometimes, you might not have a clear indication of what causes the guilt at all.

However, you need to find healthy ways to cope with this emotion before it consumes you. To ease your sense of guilt, you need to start by accepting it as a part of caregiving. Accepting the emotions that come with providing care is the first step in working through them. Part of caring for yourself emotionally includes coping with caregiver guilt, and the following guidelines will help you get started.

Notice The Feeling of Guilt

Bringing the feeling of guilt to light will help you sort through it. Strong feelings are a part of the human emotional spectrum—guilt included—and it's through noticing how you feel that you can manage the intensity of the feeling. Once you notice the feeling, allow yourself to accept it.

Identify the Cause of Guilt

Once you've sat with the feeling a bit, try and trace it back to the source. What do you think you feel guilty about? Why do you think you feel this way? Figuring out what the cause of guilt is can help you handle yourself more compassionately.

Be Kind to Yourself

Cut yourself some slack. Caregiving is not supposed to be easy and it's okay to feel certain uncomfortable feelings along the way, so be kind to yourself. Also, take a day off so you can cater to your own emotional needs.

Consider a Different Perspective

To ease the guilt, you need to consider a different perspective. Try to view your emotions and the situation in a positive light. Shift your thinking from unrealistic expectations of how things should be to a more realistic approach of embracing them as they are. Rather than focusing on the things you can't control, focus on what you can.

Get Social Support

Importantly, keep in mind that you can't do this on your own and you shouldn't have to. It's crucial to build a strong support system for yourself. Getting social support can help you keep a positive attitude toward caregiving. For example, get together with trustworthy people to vent or talk about the challenges of everything. You can also meet your friends just to relax and talk about everything else but the stress of day-to-day things. Social support is a great form of self-care, and it can boost your relationships with others.

Social Wellness: Maintaining Relationships and Connections

The unique challenges that come with dementia care can make it hard to maintain positive connections. However, it's important to stop your social life from dwindling. You need to put measures into place to make sure that you aren't going through life alone. Relationships are sacred, and investing in positive ones can change your life and perspective for the better. Social interactions can take you away from the pressure of dementia care and bring all the good things in life into focus. Maintaining relationships will help you keep some sense of normalcy, despite the difficulties around you.

Reaching out to caring people can help you maintain emotional stability and motivate a positive outlook on things. Whether you go for a coffee with your friend or socialize with a stranger at the grocery store, it's important to stay connected. Relationships are a way for you to lift your head from the demands of caregiving and notice the beauty around you.

Also, maintaining relationships keeps you socially adept because it provides a fresh perspective in your now routine-oriented life. You shouldn't be so goal-driven that you neglect to tend to the aspects of life that bring out the joy in you. Staying in contact with people is powerful, and it helps you manage your responsibilities while having extra support. Balance is everything in the life of a caregiver because things can quickly consume you if you let them. You may be wondering how you can go about staying socially healthy, and the next points will guide you.

Keeping Your Social Life as a Caregiver

Caregiving can be all-consuming, but it's important to maintain your social life as a caregiver. Making time for yourself and sustaining the things you love is the purest form of self-care. When you neglect your well-being and put your social life to the side, you risk experiencing caregiver burnout.

If you find it hard to stay active in your social life or if you notice your responsibilities get in the way of your connection, you could benefit from putting structures in place. At first, the idea of socializing can feel overwhelming like you are adding something else to your already full plate, but it's necessary. You need to establish healthy ways to stay connected so you can have a mental break from constantly providing care.

Tips to Help You Stay Connected as a Caregiver

Staying connected will boost your mood and help you keep an optimistic mindset. Spending time with friends and family can help you see things that you may miss in your day-to-day encounters as a caregiver. It can also help you unwind, as the conversations you have help you release some of the tension you might feel. Social interaction can be virtual, in-person, and over the phone; all of these options will help you feel rejuvenated. If by any chance you have no idea where or how to stay connected with people, the following tips will be helpful.

Take Advantage of Social Media Tools

When you use tools like WhatsApp, you can stay connected to the people you love most. Through social media tools, you can create an online community to provide you with the social support that you need. For example, many platforms have advocacy groups and online support teams that can give you the opportunity you need to work through your experience as a caregiver. Community is important because when you feel supported, understood, loved, and cared for you have your feelings validated. When you feel validated, you become more motivated to show up in all areas of your life. Take advantage of social media tools by installing beneficial applications on your phone to help you take better care of yourself while building connections with other people. Social wellness is just as important as all other forms of well-being. Social media is a chance to keep a healthy level of social connection as you maintain contact with groups and individuals. You can even start your blog to share your thoughts about dementia care so others can learn and feel connected to your experience. Getting things out in a safe space and hearing other people's experiences can help you relax and prevent caregiver exhaustion. Of all the ways you could use social media, make sure it's to your advantage.

Plan Social Time

Socializing and staying connected to people will help you feel less alone in your life, so you need to plan social time. Plan dates and visits with your friends days or weeks in advance so you always have something to look forward to. Even plan social time with your family like doing bonding activities over the weekend. In tandem with making time for yourself, building social connections will improve your health. Be sure to do something fun with the people you love at least once a week. Planning social time also means not canceling plans unless it's an emergency. Caregiving can consume, thus, convince you to put your social connections on the back burner, but it's important to push past the temptation to continuously cancel plans. Social time is essential because it minimizes feelings of depression and helplessness while increasing feelings of nurture and happiness.

Talk To People Who Get You

In caregiving, you spend most of your time catering to others. Your social circle should be the one time you feel understood and catered to. This means creating a circle of support filled with people who want to understand you. People who "get you" should feel like a safe space for you to share your deepest vulnerabilities. You should be able to talk to your people about the stressors of caregiving without feeling judged or labeled for it. The people who understand you will improve your day as you communicate with them. Each time you are with the people who support you should leave you feeling encouraged. Your people should be able to give you constructive criticism so you can grow from your mistakes rather than feel condemned for them. You are incredible and the people in your life should see and support that too.

Stay in Contact Frequently

Your social connections will demand that you stay active in people's lives as you want them to remain active in yours. This means, prioritizing staying in contact with people frequently. For example, short phone calls or quick texts will go a long way. Being in contact with loved ones can prove the bit of joy you need during a tough day. People can also offer you a sense of comfort and humor when you need it most. When you stay in contact frequently, it also shows the other person that you care for them even when life gets busy. Staying in contact shows that you appreciate the connections you've made regardless of how difficult things can get.

Self-care is all about keeping your mind and body in check, and that means knowing when you need to ask for help. Part of staying socially well is seeking professional assistance. No one is meant to go through life alone, so getting support from therapists and groups is important; this will be explored next.

Seeking Professional Help: Therapy and Support Groups

Caregiver burnout is a real thing that therapy can help you navigate. Seeking professional help will also provide you with the tools you need to manage the demands of caregiving. Being a caregiver can take an immense toll on your emotional health, physical well-being, and social wellness if you neglect them. However, getting into therapy and having support from social groups can offer you quality self-care.

The professional help provided in therapy and from social support groups makes it possible for you to work through complex emotions and feelings of being overwhelmed. Professionals also know better than friends and family about how to help you navigate mental health issues and maintain good health. Besides, the information about how stressful caregiving is can be overwhelming to share with the people closest to you. Sometimes they may not have the solutions to help you overcome the obstacles, but professionals are trained to help you through such challenges.

Why Counseling Is Important for Caregivers

According to *The Importance of Counseling for Caregivers* (n.d.), mental health disorders are more common among dementia caregivers compared to any other group. Hence, counseling is important to help reduce the number of caregivers who suffer from mental health issues as it relates to caregiving. The pressure of dementia care has been said to increase depression and anxiety with 34% and 44% of caregivers reporting experiencing depression and anxiety, respectively (*The Importance of Counseling for Caregivers*, n.d.). Even though not all caregivers will experience mental health issues, a significant enough number of people in caregiving do struggle with it so the topic is important to explore.

Counseling caregivers can help identify whether they are prone to mental health battles or not. Also, discovering mental health struggles early can help facilitate positive ways to cope and overcome the battle. Counseling also prevents the feeling of isolation when experiencing these issues. Too often, people who aren't caregivers or professionals may not understand why caregivers feel anxious or depressed, but therapy gives a safe space for this understanding to be facilitated. In situations where caregivers feel disempowered or helpless, professional help offers solutions to overcome difficulties.

A trained therapist will help you process strong emotions, learn coping mechanisms, improve communication, strengthen your problem-solving skills, and enhance boundaries so you can care for and receive care from others. Whether in-person, online, or through other discussions, counseling provides the type of emotional support that caregivers can benefit from.

Therapy for Caregivers: Options and Opportunities

Therapy is a chance to feel heard and supported by someone who has studied the emotional stages of your experience. When you share with a therapist they are bound by law to keep your conversations confidential, so that means you can freely get things off your chest privately and without the fear of judgment. Working through things with a counselor also helps in the following ways:

- **Emotional relief:** When you start therapy, it gives you the tools you need to overcome mental blocks and feel empowered as a caregiver. The empowerment you gain from the professional experience will bring you emotional relief like no other. You get to leave everything in the hands of good counsel, and you may be pleased to learn that most of the things you experience are fairly common challenges in dementia care.

- **Improve interpersonal skills:** Offloading with a professional helps you gain coping mechanisms so you can show up as a better, non-complaining version of yourself. When you are unburdened, it is generally much easier to communicate with other people in a healthy, nonprojecting way. Therapy gives you the space to learn more about yourself and overcome tough situations, so you can take those skills into personal interactions. When you are happier and healthier your interpersonal connections thrive too.

- **Confront the uncomfortable:** It's easy to brush things under the rug when you don't have to communicate them. If anything, it's human nature to want to avoid the awkwardness of vulnerability; so, you'll find yourself hiding some of your feelings about caregiving for the sake of appearing a certain way in social settings. However, therapists will get to the root of all your worries and concerns. When you are in session, you are encouraged to confront the uncomfortable feelings, thoughts, and problems that you may be inclined to avoid most times. Counseling is an opportunity to talk about the tough subjects that you might avoid sharing with your family and friends.

- **Receive nonjudgmental and objective feedback.** The best part about confiding in a therapist is that they can provide constructive feedback based on what they've observed during sessions. You can receive nonjudgmental and objective feedback to improve your personal and professional life altogether.

A healthier you is more productive, energetic, and happy, that's what therapy will provide for you. Of course, you get to decide what type of therapy would work in your situation. From a vast number of options, you get to choose what works.

Options For Therapy

Several options exist for therapy, so there's no excuse to avoid going. When you find what speaks to your lifestyle and schedule, you will be set to receive regular professional support.

Individual Therapy for Caregivers

One-on-one or individual therapy focuses on tailored conversations and emotional support. The individual therapy option gives you a private space to confide in your therapist without anyone else weighing in. It's all about you and the emotions or experiences that you have to share. Typically, individual therapy helps you hone in on your strengths and improve in areas where you are most reactive. Individual therapy can enhance your caregiving role and help you regulate your emotions.

Family Therapy for Caregivers

Alternatively, the second option is family therapy. This form of therapy is more about bettering yourself through the health of a collective. Family therapy seeks to improve communication and bonds between family members. This can be extremely beneficial to families who are battling a dementia diagnosis. During family therapy sessions, each member of the family collaborates with the therapist to come up with valuable solutions that can help the unit. Family therapy focuses on uncovering and working through problems within the family dynamic that can hinder individual growth. The primary goal is to address things that can interfere with the caregiver's ability to perform their duties compassionately as well as identify ways to create a healthier, more helpful family structure.

Group Therapy for Caregivers

Professional counselors and therapists generally conduct group sessions. Their training in the field allows a group of caregivers to share experiences, exercises, and activities geared toward self-improvement. Each person in the group is encouraged to share about their unique encounters during caregiving to subsequently receive support from other caregivers.

Group therapy can be an optimal choice for you, especially if you feel awkward having to talk to a professional by yourself. Dong therapy in a group setting can help you realize that you aren't alone because there is a team of caregivers who need support as much as you do. Group therapy also helps you build trust with people who have similar encounters, so your feelings and struggles can be met with empathy. In group sessions, you and other caregivers can learn the commonalities in dementia care and discover ways to cope.

Pastoral Care for Caregivers

Finally, option four leans more into the spiritual aspect of counseling. Pastoral care incorporates therapy, connection with your faith, and the community into providing you with holistic support. Here, you get to view your problems as a caregiver through the lens of theology or other spiritual beliefs. Faith can be comforting for many people because it adds meaning to life. Whether you believe in God, the Universe, or other spiritual components, pastoral care can be beneficial to your healing. Receiving care from people who you have a spiritual connection with can help you grow in the right direction and uncover far deeper parts of yourself.

Self-care aims to prevent falling into despair and losing yourself due to the pressure of caregiving. Self-care allows you to overcome difficulties so you can be a better caregiver and overall person. You are important, and self-care is a way to ensure that your health is not sacrificed in your attempt to help other people navigate their own.

Burnout has been a topic of discussion in this chapter, mainly how self-care can help prevent it. However, you could benefit from receiving more information about this phenomenon, and the next chapter does that.

CHAPTER 7

Preventing Caregiver Burnout–Strategies for Long-Term Resilience

It's not how much we give, but how much love we put into giving.

–Mother Teresa

Dementia care is stressful, especially when you make no time to take care of yourself. Caregiver burnout happens when the stress of caregiving catches up with you. It's when the experience of caring for someone leaves you feeling physically, emotionally, and mentally overwhelmed and exhausted. You might feel lonely, unappreciated, and unsupported on more days than one. The lack of self-care in your routine may mean that you feel depressed and extremely anxious in response to caregiver burnout. Experiencing burnout may even cause you to lose interest in caregiving as well as in self-caring. The good news is that caregiver burnout is preventable with the correct measures in place.

Most caregivers are likely to experience caregiver burnout at some point. If you feel fatigue and you don't address it immediately or know what the early signs are, you may find yourself headed toward burnout. Preventing caregiver burnout is to help you avoid the pitfalls of such fatigue so you can continue to provide quality self-care and caregiving. The main point of this chapter is to help you see the signs of caregiver burnout so you can prevent it. Here, you'll get techniques on how to manage caregiver stress through breathing, relaxation, and mindfulness activities.

Recognizing the Warning Signs of Caregiver Burnout

According to *Signs of Caregiver Burnout and How to Prevent It* (n.d.), you might be one of 40 million people in America who provide care. Whether the caregiving is out of obligation, profession, or love, it can put you and millions of others at risk for burnout. The unrelieved mental, physical, and emotional stress of caregiving shouldn't be taken lightly. In the field of psychology and mental health, caregiver burnout is recognized as the symptom of unrelieved stress that begins to affect the well-being of caregivers. A myriad of factors may contribute to the experience of caregiver burnout, some of which go beyond the stress of providing care itself. For example, you may be in a state of constant worry about financial pressures and dementia progression. It might be difficult for you to fully comprehend the illness that you are now charged to care for. When these worries are permitted to continue unmanaged, it is a recipe for caregiver burnout that could put you and the people in care at risk.

Think of caregiver burnout as being the outcome of lighting your candle on both ends. You become so focused on providing care for others that you forget or neglect to take care of yourself along the way. However, recognizing the signs of caregiver burnout puts you in a position where you can solve or prevent it.

The Signs of Caregiver Burnout

Some of the warning signs include:

- Feelings of anxiety

- Lack of concentration

- Low energy

- Feelings of exhaustion

- A sense of losing control

- Lack of emotional balance

- Limited self-care

- High irritability

- Loss of interest in things you enjoy

- Feelings of hopelessness and depression

- Being overwhelmed

- Low resistance to physical illness

- Self-neglect

Caregiver burnout can lead to physical symptoms such as body aches, loss or increase of appetite, unusual changes in weight, trouble sleeping, and frequent headaches. As caregiver burnout progresses, so will the negative effects on the mind and body. If you find yourself leaning toward unhealthy stress relievers such as drugs, overworking, and alcohol, you might already be in a dangerous spot. You need help to overcome the signs of burnout, and stress management tools can help you do that.

Most importantly, remember that it's important to teach yourself to ask for help and receive it. Caregiver burnout can happen when you avoid asking for help in areas where you need it. Your mind may convince you that you can do things on your own. Though that could be true, it's also a very unsustainable way to live. Having trouble asking for help or accepting support from other people is a huge sign that you are headed to burnout. Below are stress management tools to help you cope with the signs of burnout, and hopefully, permit yourself to ask for a helping hand when you need it.

Stress Management Strategies

Getting strategies to manage stress immediately will help you prevent caregiver burnout. Learning new strategies to help you manage stress is integral to your health, and some of these are as simple as asking for help.

Simple Strategies for Stress Prevention

Once you are aware of the signs of caregiver burnout, it's time to intervene for yourself and treat the fatigue that comes from it. Recognize that there are plenty of things you can do to keep yourself healthy, safe, cared for, and burnout averse; let's take a look.

Seek Help

Talking about the stress of caregiving and seeking help from people who get it is vital. People around you can help you process the emotions that come with caregiving so you can prevent yourself from being overwhelmed by them. Asking for help is one of the most beneficial things you can do for yourself as a caregiver. Being open to receiving help from others is an underrated way to prevent caregiver burnout. Support also enables you to release some of the emotional tension you might feel by sharing your story with others just like you, or those who simply care about your well-being.

Prioritize Personal Care and Fitness

Asking for help prioritizes what you need. Taking personal care and fitness into consideration should keep you above board and away from burnout. Personal care involves being kind to yourself and doing more of the things that bring you joy. It's also about taking breaks when you need them while maintaining social activities such as cycling, yoga, or team-building. When you refuse to lose yourself in the field of caregiving, you protect yourself from feeling tired over time. Remember to eat healthy, exercise, and practice the things you enjoy. Caregiving shouldn't be your only focus; instead, you should permit yourself to live a robust life that keeps you feeling balanced and healthy.

Consider Respite Care

If you need a couple of hours to yourself and a break from caregiving, respite care is the answer. This type of care suggests getting a home care aide or substitute care for the time you are away just to give you some breathing space. Respite care involves taking the person who has dementia to a care facility for a day, or even hiring someone to take over responsibility while you take a break. However, respite care does require additional expenses that might not be covered by medical insurance. If you are considering respite care, you also need to prepare for it financially.

Keeping a healthy spirit, body, and mind is essential for your caregiver toolkit. Using stress management strategies for stress relief provides a resource for you to overcome burnout warning signs. Next, you will get some breathing techniques to help you manage stress. Calming breathwork usually takes just a few minutes to help you through the stress. Also, breathing techniques can be done anywhere and anytime to help you relieve stress.

Breathing Strategies for Stress Relief

Doing breathing techniques as part of your daily routine can benefit you immensely. You can do breathing techniques while sitting up, lying down, or stretching out on a yoga mat in the comfort of your floor. Even if you are at work, you can grab your office chair and practice breathing strategies.

Before you begin any breathing strategy you need to make yourself as comfortable as you can. Your legs can be straight or you can have bent knees as you firmly position yourself on the surface beneath you. If you are sitting, then put your arms on the chair rest, and place your feet hip-distance wide on the floor. Always allow your breath to flow deeply down your body into your lungs without forcing the breath to pass through you. Remember to take gentle, intentional breaths.

Breath Focus Strategy

The first breathing strategy that you can consider is breath focus. This technique uses imagery or words and phrases that can help you feel centered. You can choose a simple phrase or focus word that makes you happy. The aim is to create an environment of relaxation by using this word and your breath to keep things neutral. Some great focus words or phrases include "stay calm," "release," "let go," and "be at peace." However, you can choose any word or phrase that fits the context you are in. Your choice must align with your intention for that breath focus.

Now, move on to the breathing part of the strategy. You can start with 5–10-minute sessions, and gradually increase the number of time you spend doing the technique as you get familiar with it. Breath focus can take at least 20 minutes when you get the hang of it (Cronkleton, 2023). The steps for breath focus are:

1. Get into a comfortable position. Either lie down or sit up in a way that's unforced and feels most natural to you.

2. Bring awareness to your body, breath, and intention. To start the breathing, you need to first ground your mind in the awareness that the technique is happening.

3. Take normal, intentional breaths for the first minute or two of your practice. Breathe in and out to get what your natural rhythm is.

4. Now, alternate between your usual pattern of breathing to taking deeper, longer breaths. Notice the differences between your natural breath style and the deeper pattern. Bring awareness to your stomach as your lungs inflate with oxygen, and then deflate as you exhale.

5. Pay attention to the shallowness of your natural breath compared to the depth of deep breathing. When you are ready and have taken a mental note of these differences, you can shift your breathing style to deep breaths. Do intentional, gradual, long, and deep inhalations as well as exhalations, and feel how this changes your body.

6. Then, place your dominant hand right below your belly button. Remain calm and relaxed as you notice the rise and fall of your tummy. Be sure to feel the sensation of your belly movement through your hand.

7. When you are ready, let out a loud and freeing sigh each time you exhale. Repeat that for about five complete sighs.

8. Get ready to combine your deep breaths with imagery or a focus word that supports your relaxation. You can say the word right after your sigh and immediately before you draw your next big breath. For example, take a deep breath in, exhale with a loud sigh, and then proceed to whisper "let go" under your breath before drawing the next.

9. Imagine the flow of air rushing through your body as you inhale, and imagine it covering you with warmth as you exhale. Allow the breath to bring you a sense of calmness that you can't get anywhere else. Remind yourself in this moment that you are inhaling peace and exhaling stress.

10. Imagine the flow of air leaving your body is brushing tension and stress right off of you. Remind yourself that you are exhaling all the negative, overwhelming things and inhaling all the restorative ones.

Breath focus is about being attentive to your breath as you guide it for your purposes. If you lose focus on your words or imagery, don't panic, it happens. Instead, carefully return your attention to your breath and continue the technique.

Deep Breathing for Stress Relief

Deep breathing is a stress relief strategy that prevents air from getting trapped in your lungs. It helps you mitigate shortness of breath and shallow breathing. When you use the deep breathing strategy you begin to breathe in fresh air and increase your lung capacity. Deep breathing is a great way to promote relaxation and groundedness. You can practice deep breathing by:

1. Choosing a relaxing position. You can sit or stand, then draw your elbows back to open up your chest a bit more. This will allow you to take advantage of your chest cavities and permit more air to flow through your body.

2. Breathe deeply through your nose.

3. Hold your breath for five counts.

4. Then, gradually exhale through your nose.

5. Repeat.

If you experience any dizziness or alarming sensations throughout your body, stop the practice immediately. Always do breathing techniques that feel good for your body and where you feel supported. The best way to choose an exercise that works for you is to focus on attempting all of the suggested techniques before making your decision about which one works for you.

Diaphragmatic Breathing for Stress Relief

Diaphragmatic breathing is also known as belly breathing, and it can help you use your stomach muscles to optimize your breath. Belly breathing helps manage respiratory challenges and heart issues, and reduces stress. You can do diaphragmatic breathing for 5 to 10 minutes and at least three times per day (Cronkleton, 2023). Initially, belly breathing can feel tiring and hard, but it gets easier with practice and time. To start the practice, you can use the next steps as guidance:

1. Lie on your back with slightly bent knees and lay your head on your pillow. You may benefit from using another pillow under your knees for additional support.

2. Place your dominant hand on your upper chest area and the less dominant hand under your ribcage. Permit yourself to feel the movement of your muscles as you breathe. Be sure to activate your stomach muscles with each inhalation, don't be afraid of what your breaths look like. Remember, this is less about appearance and more about the practice itself.

3. Inhale slowly through your nose as you feel your stomach rise and pressure builds into your hand. Do

your best to keep your hands as still and centered as you possibly can.

4. Then, exhale as if to tighten your stomach muscles to squeeze every bit of breath out of your body. As you exhale, tighten your lips together for more of a controlled exercise. Keep the hand on your chest and as still as possible while the one on your stomach moves up and down to the rhythm of your breath.

To make the practice even more interesting you can use a book and place it on your abdomen as you breathe. When you can master your breathing in the laid-back position, you can then try to sit up in your chair to increase the difficulty. Once you master that, go a step further by introducing belly breathing as part of daily activities.

Equal Breathing for Stress Relief

In meditation practice, equal breathing is known as Sama Vritti (Cronkleton, 2023). The equal breathing strategy for stress relief focuses on keeping a balance between your inhalations and exhalations so you can perform steady breaths. A study on adults with health conditions such as the risk of high blood pressure shows that the equal breathing technique improves your oxygen supply (Noventi et al., 2022). It also helps you feel mentally well and physically refreshed. To start the practice you can follow the following steps for guidance:

1. Take a seat and feel comfortable.

2. Inhale then exhale through your nose.

3. Feel free to count during each inhalation and exhalation to ensure that you have an equal duration of breaths on each. You can also include a phrase or word to make the practice more intentional for you.

4. Include a pause between your inhalation and exhalation to mimic the rhythm of normal breathing. So, inhale until your lungs are at capacity and then pause. Once you are at the top of your breath exhale the same number of counts. Make sure that you stay comfortable and calm throughout.

5. Keep doing the practice for at least five minutes.

Equal breathing is good for your brain and lungs, especially when you use a balanced technique to breathe. You can take about three to five breath counts to maintain your calmness throughout the practice. First, master the technique of equal breaths in a stationary position; for example, do it while sitting. Once you get the hang of it in that position, you can start to do it during physical movement and activity.

Resonant Breathing for Stress Relief

When you breathe coherently it's known as resonant breathing. For example, breathe in to the count of three using your breath as reference, then exhale to the count of three. Resonant breath is about taking full, controlled breaths per minute to help you find a sweet spot for relaxation. Breathing air using this strategy optimizes your heart rate variability (HRV), minimizes anxiety, and helps you manage stress (Cronkleton, 2023). At some point, combining breathing with exercise eventually helps you feel better and less depressed. To do this exercise you can follow the next steps:

1. Manage your inhalation to the count of five.

2. Exhale to the count of five.

3. Then, continue the pattern for a few more minutes.

Reducing caregiver stress will prevent burnout and help you be more productive and helpful in multiple areas of your life. Receiving help, support, and self-care are all strategies for stress management that can help you feel like you desire the demands of caregiving. Your well-being is important as without it you can't do anything, so you need to put things into place to ensure that you are taken care of.

If you have any preexisting conditions, it's important to include your doctor in the decision-making process. Also, consult a respiratory counselor or breathwork teacher to learn more about breathing strategies. On the topic of relaxation, mindfulness is an exercise that helps.

The Role of Mindfulness and Relaxation

Dementia caregivers and family members can benefit from mindfulness-based stress reduction exercises. Practicing mindfulness is a form of meditation that can improve blood circulation and pressure, increase cognitive functioning, and reduce stress reactivity (Boxtel et al., 2020). Mindfulness plays a significant role in relaxation and stress management.

What Is Mindfulness?

The act of being fully present and aware of your thoughts, surroundings, actions, and feelings while not being consumed by them is mindfulness. You can see what's going on around you without letting it affect your peace and stability. Mindfulness is important in dementia care because it helps you bring awareness to your emotional experiences as well as the situations that may trigger them so you can take control of your moments. Being mindful is all about honoring your feelings and the situations you are confronted by without feeling the need to judge or change the experience.

Exercising mindfulness involves a range of techniques that promote relaxation and calmness. For example, guided imagery and breathing strategies are two of many mindfulness-based practices. The stress management strategies that you engage in from the book are valuable examples of mindfulness at work. Essentially, being mindful is being present with all of your feelings and thoughts but not allowing yourself to be overcome. This practice helps to redirect your focus from thoughts of worry to simply letting yourself engage with the experience.

As a caregiver, you can practice mindfulness by using the stress management strategies in the book. Also, permitting yourself to get the full experience in everything you do is a form of being mindful. Since mindfulness is about accepting your experiences for what they are, it can be practiced anywhere. For example, revive your awareness during mealtimes; a sense of presence can involve paying attention to the taste, smell, and texture of your food when you eat. An act as simple as being attentive to activities like eating, breathing, or drinking can restore your balance and peace. Mindfulness is beneficial in numerous ways.

The Benefits of Mindfulness

Evidence supports that mindfulness can help caregivers relieve tension and feel more rested (Meditation Tips for Caregiver Mindfulness, n.d.). When you practice being mindful it can help you appreciate your life more. Additional benefits of being mindful include:

- Better sleep patterns

- Greater memory and attentiveness

- Feeling happier and less burned out

- Feeling centered and aware of your emotions (being emotionally regulated)

Practicing mindfulness triggers relaxation in the body and mind by reducing stress and helping you take in the full experience of being alive. Mindfulness is about paying attention and being the main character of your life, rather than letting things control you as you take a passive interest.

How to Practice Mindfulness as a Caregiver

As previously mentioned, one of the greatest things about mindfulness is that it can be practiced anywhere and at any time. So caregivers can practice noticing emotions without judgment at any point during the day. To practice mindfulness you simply need to get into the habit of taking stock of the goodness and the unpleasant experiences that surround you. It's about being aware of personal emotions and how you react to them. Mindful presence requires you to slow down and be attentive to your senses: What do you hear? What do you see? How do you feel? What can you smell? Is there something you can taste? If so, appreciate the pleasures that come with noticing where you are and how you feel. For example, if you notice that you feel a cool breeze over your skin, consider how your body reacts to it. Allow yourself to be immersed in the experience and be grateful for the fact that you can feel it.

You may want to include the questions from above in your breathing exercises when you are ready. Always pay attention to sensations, feelings, and movements. During mindful practice, you need to take your time to go through the flow. Make sure you aren't forcing yourself to find or feel things, rather be receptive to what's already there. With this level of acceptance and observation, you will likely get better at being mindful over time.

Progressive Muscle Relaxation

Of the many types of meditations, progressive muscle relaxation can be integrated into your routine to help you feel more settled within yourself. Progressive muscle relaxation is a type of mindfulness meditation that brings awareness to each part of your body. It's about bringing your attention from external things into the inward environment. Progressive muscle relaxation allows you to move your attention from your toes up to your head. Focus on what your body is feeling as you breathe through the practice. You need to tense one part of your body at a time to bring your mind's focus to it, then release it to see if you notice any tension that may linger long after you've relaxed.

Your body, like everyone else's, can hold large chunks of tension, so this practice can help you let go. Focus on one limb and muscle area at a time, contract and release, and then allow for a pause so you can take account of how you feel in the moment. Tense the current area of focus as you inhale, then release with every exhale. Feel free to be loud in your breathing because the practice doesn't have to look pretty, it just needs to feel good. You need to give yourself the space you need to be completely mindful. The practice of being aware is a way to take care of yourself and prevent burnout.

The Significance of Establishing Healthy Boundaries

Boundaries are rules of personal conduct that you set for yourself to teach people how to treat you. Setting good boundaries is beneficial as it saves you from situations of overextending yourself or being mistreated by people who are constantly expecting something of you. Boundaries are essential to your well-being as a caregiver because you are so busy prioritizing the needs of others, and it can drain you without them. Setting boundaries is a way of taking care of yourself, and making sure that you don't drain yourself in the process of caregiving.

A boundary is recognizing that your space, energy, and resources need to be protected. It's the ability to say, "no" without feeling guilty for protecting your peace. Boundaries outline what you are available for and what you aren't willing to do, and setting these clear expectations will improve your relationships as well as your abilities as a caregiver.

Set Your Boundaries

Setting boundaries can look unique for each person because what you find acceptable may be different from the next person. Boundaries can be difficult to set because as a giver, your natural position is to want to be there for people and to provide help when you can. However, if you continue to give at your own expense, it will be detrimental in the long term. Some general points to consider in your boundary-setting journey are listed below.

Clarify Your Needs

Set your boundaries specific to every area of your life that requires your energy and effort. Your job, relationships, and home life should all have boundaries to help you feel protected. To set clear boundaries you merely need to highlight what you want, so you can reject anything that goes against that desire. For example, if you want breaks during a busy work day, you might set a boundary around this. So you may tell your co-workers and family that you aren't available around a certain time of the day because it is your break time. Once you've clarified your boundary, stick to it and stand up for yourself.

Say "No" Decisively

Part of setting boundaries is developing the ability to say "no" when you feel someone is asking more of you than you are willing to give. For example, if your family member is supposed to take on the next shift but provides a superficial reason to get you to stay longer, simply say "no." You can make your boundaries clear by rejecting any proposals that go against the grain of what you want. Take the example above about breaks, saying "no" in that context could be to a person who refuses to honor your boundary. For instance, someone at work may try to convince you to take on extra responsibility during your break times. You may communicate, "I won't be available for that, I'm on break," but that person may continue to push. In this context, your "no" is enough. You can clearly state that you feel like you've made your boundary clear and they should not expect you to be available to take on that responsibility at that time.

Be Wise About Your Availability, Access, and Time

So many people will want access to you, thus, attempting to convince you to go against your boundaries to benefit themselves. However, you need to learn to only do things that are important for your well-being and success. Even in helping people, make sure that it realistically falls within your wheelhouse of abilities. For example, you don't have to attend an optional work event if you already have family plans.

Also, the people you spend time with are important. You need to be intentional about what and who is worth your energy and effort. People can either pour into your life or cause you to feel drained, so be picky about who you sit around with. Caregiving is already such a difficult responsibility, and you don't need to add the pressure of being accessible to everyone.

Communicate Your Boundaries

Once you've set your boundaries, you need to learn how to communicate them to others. Boundaries are to establish a clear line between what's acceptable and unacceptable to you, and they need to be communicated respectfully, compassionately, and assertively. The next person needs to be as clear about your limitations as you are in making them.

Part of communicating your boundaries is always ensuring that your needs are still being catered to in the decisions you are making. For example, if your boss keeps trying to reach you after work hours you can be clear by saying, "I will only be available for this when work starts tomorrow." Communicate that you are not willing to accept extra work outside of your standing work hours. While it might not always feel good to communicate boundaries, particularly to friends and family, it is necessary.

Things You Can Do When Boundaries are Violated

Now, there will be instances where your communication is undermined or dismissed. However, there are things you can do when your boundaries are violated to ensure that people either start respecting the rules you've set or lose access to you altogether. Take the example of your boss trying to reach after hours. If that persistence continues despite your clear reasoning behind not answering work commitments outside of work hours, then you can just disable your email notifications after work. Doing this will ensure that you aren't being bombarded with alerts about what needs to be done during personal hours.

Setting, communicating, and advocating for personal boundaries will save you a lot of disappointment and prevent burnout. Boundaries allow you to decide what's worth your time and what is not. These also ensure that your energy is spent according to your priority list. With all of these tips and tricks, dementia care can feel more manageable than ever.

Conclusion

Whether it's financially, physically, or by being supportive, you should be proud of your ability to care for others. Dementia care is something that strikes many families with elderly members, you aren't alone. It's important to give yourself the gift of self-belief as you try to understand what you're working through.

The experience of caring for someone with dementia can differ as the condition progresses. However, the information in this book gives you the strategies and knowledge you need to prepare yourself for what's coming. The value of this book is to help you become a better supporter in the caregiving area that you need to show up in. Every bit of information can be put into action, from understanding the different symptoms associated with dementia behavior to learning how to stay compassionate along the way. It's all about knowing that there's a way to care for your patients or loved ones with gentleness while caring for yourself in the process.

Self-care and setting boundaries are the core components of any healthy individual. For you to show up productively and provide compassionate dementia care, your needs must be met. You can't avoid yourself as a sacrifice to help others. If anything, caregiving is more about taking note of what you need so you can be better at spotting the next person's needs as well.

REFERENCES

AARP. (2019, October 31). *Dementia care: helping your loved one stay connected and safe.* Family Caregiving. https://www.aarp.org/caregiving/basics/info-2019/alzheimers-dementia-care.html

A healthy diet can help caregivers reduce stress. (2020, October 23). Adult Family Care. https://adultfamilycare.org/a-healthy-diet-can-help-caregivers-reduce-stress/

Aducanumab approved for treatment of Alzheimer's disease. (n.d.). Alzheimer's Association. https://www.alz.org/alzheimers-dementia/treatments/aducanumab

Aging, dementia, and Alzheimer's–Medicare and Medigap assistance. Blue California. https://www.blueshieldca.com/bsca/bsc/wcm/connect/sites/Sites_Content_EN/medicare/learn-about-medicare/medicaretopics/medicare-article-cards/aging_dementia_alzheimers

Alexy, J. (2018, August 7). *How to set boundaries as a caregiver.* Aegis Living. https://www.aegisliving.com/resource-center/set-boundaries-as-a-caregiver/

Allen, K. (2021, July 8). *Developing a dementia care plan.* Alzheimer's Diseases Research. https://www.brightfocus.org/alzheimers/article/developing-dementia-care-plan

Alsawy, S., Tai, S., McEvoy, P., & Mansell, W. (2020). 'It's nice to think somebody's listening to me instead of saying "oh shut up." People with dementia reflect on what makes communication good and meaningful. *Journal of psychiatric and mental health nursing, 27(2),* 151–161. https://doi.org/10.1111/jpm.12559

Alzheimer's disease facts and figures. (n.d.). Alzheimer's Association. https://www.alz.org/alzheimers-dementia/facts-figures?utm_source=google&utm_medium=paidsearch&utm_campaign=google_grants&utm_content=alzheimers&gclid=Cj0KCQjwnbmaBhD-ARIsAGTPcfXmqb6CGYTES_9v5DNuBv3qysnx3AvVxf-Qt-EtkpSxU4eqBK14UYcaAi8HEALw_wcB

Anxiety and agitation. (n.d.). Alzheimer's Association. https://www.alz.org/help-support/caregiving/stages-behaviors/anxiety-agitation

Assistive technology for dementia. (n.d.). The Good Care Group. https://www.thegoodcaregroup.com/live-in-care/dementia-care/assistive-technology-for-dementia/

Behavior in dementia as a form of communication. (2020, October). Social Care Institute of Excellence. https://www.scie.org.uk/dementia/after-diagnosis/communication/behaviour.asp

Bojaxhiu, M.T., MC. (n.d.). *Quote by Mother Teresa.* GoodReads. https://www.goodreads.com/quotes/20324-it-s-not-how-much-we-give-but-how-much-love

Boxtel, M. P, J., Berk, L., de Vugt, M. E., & van Warmenhoven, F. (2020). *Mindfulness-based interventions for people with dementia and their caregivers: keeping a dyadic balance.* Taylor & Francis Online. https://www.tandfonline.com/doi/full/10.1080/13607863.2019.1582004

Breathing exercises for stress. (n.d.). NHS. https://www.nhs.uk/mental-health/self-help/guides-tools-and-activities/breathing-exercises-for-stress/

Caregiver burnout. (n.d.). Cleveland Clinic. https://my.clevelandclinic.org/health/diseases/9225-caregiver-burnout

Carrarini, C., Russo, M., Dono, F., Barbone, F., Rispoli, M. G., Ferri, L., Di Pietro, M., Digiovanni, A., Ajdinaj, P., Speranza, R., Granzotto, A., Frazzini, V., Thomas, A., Pilotto, A., Padovani, A., Onofrj, M., Sensi, S. L., & Bonanni, L. (2021). Agitation and dementia: prevention and treatment strategies in acute and chronic conditions. *Frontiers in Neurology, 12,* 644317. https://doi.org/10.3389/fneur.2021.644317

Cherished Companions. (2019, October 14). *Dementia care: a caregiver's guide to supporting patients with compassion.* Cherish Agency. https://cherishedagency.com/dementia-care-caregivers-guide/

Communication and Alzheimer's. (n.d.). Alzheimer's Association. https://www.alz.org/help-support/caregiving/daily-care/communications

Communicating with people living with dementia. (n.d.). Alzheimer's Society. https://alzheimer.ca/en/help-support/i-have-friend-or-family-member-who-lives-dementia/communicating-people-living-dementia

Communicating with someone with dementia. (n.d.). NHS. https://www.nhs.uk/conditions/dementia/living-with-dementia/communication/

Communicating with a person living with a dementia. (n.d.). NiDirect. https://www.nidirect.gov.uk/articles/communicating-person-living-dementia

Coping with GP appointments when you have dementia. (n.d.). Alzheimer's Society. https://www.alzheimers.org.uk/get-support/help-with-dementia-care/tips-dementia-going-see-gp

Coping with memory loss. (n.d.). Alzheimer's Society. https://www.alzheimers.org.uk/get-support/staying-independent/coping-with-memory-loss

Cronkleton, E. (2023, March 24). *10 breathing techniques for stress relief and more.* Healthline. https://www.healthline.com/health/breathing-exercise#belly-breathing

Daily care plan. (n.d.). Alzheimer's Association. https://www.alz.org/help-support/caregiving/daily-care/daily-care-plan

DailyCaring Editorial Team. (n.d.). *15 Quick tips for managing caregiver stress.* DailyCaring. https://dailycaring.com/15-quick-tips-for-managing-caregiver-stress/

Davis, J. (2022, February 22). *Understanding the costs of dementia care.* North River Home Care. https://www.northriverhc.com/understanding-the-costs-of-dementia-care/

Dementia–behaviour changes. (n.d.). Better Health. https://www.betterhealth.vic.gov.au/health/conditionsandtreatments/dementia-behaviour-changes#hoarding-in-dementia

Dementia–early signs. (n.d.). Better Health. https://www.betterhealth.vic.gov.au/health/conditionsandtreatments/dementia-early-signs

Dementia and hiding, hoarding, or losing things. (n.d.). Alzheimer's Society. https://www.alzheimers.org.uk/about-dementia/symptoms-and-diagnosis/symptoms/hiding-hoarding-losing

Dementia with Lewy bodies. (n.d.). Alzheimer's Association. https://www.alz.org/alzheimers-dementia/what-is-dementia/types-of-dementia/dementia-with-lewy-bodies

Dementia quotes. (n.d.). Brainy Quotes. https://www.brainyquote.com/quotes/laurie_graham_687646?src=t_dementia

Erardy, A. (2021, November 22). *How mindfulness can help caregivers cope with stress and burnout.* Oncology Nursing News. https://www.oncnursingnews.com/view/how-mindfulness-can-help-caregivers-cope-with-stress-and-burnout

Exercise for caregiver health and well-being. (n.d.). Family Caregiver Alliance. https://www.caregiver.org/news/exercise-caregiver-health-and-well-being/

Exercising when you're caring for someone else. (2014, July 31). AARP. https://www.aarp.org/caregiving/life-balance/info-2017/find-time-for-exercise.html

Five lessons in setting boundaries that every caregiver must learn. Daughterhood. https://daughterhood.org/5-lessons-in-setting-boundaries-that-every-caregiver-must-learn/

Food and eating. (n.d.). Alzheimer's Association. https://www.alz.org/help-support/caregiving/daily-care/food-eating

Four things you can do to alleviate caregiver stress. (2016, October 17). Harvard Health Publishing. https://www.health.harvard.edu/staying-healthy/4-things-you-can-do-to-alleviate-caregiver-stress

Giebel, C., Halpin, K., Tottie, J., & Carton, J. (2023). The digitalization of finance management skills in dementia since the COVID-19 pandemic: A qualitative study. *Dementia (London, England),* 22(4), 783-806. https://doi.org/10.1177/14713012231159156

Graham, L. (n.d.). *Quote by Laurie Graham.* BrainyQuote. https://www.brainyquote.com/quotes/laurie_graham_687646

Hamilton, J. M. (2014, September 30). *Building caregiver resilience: Nutritional strategies for caregivers.* GrisWorld. https://www.griswoldhomecare.com/blog/2014/september/building-caregiver-resilience-nutritional-strate/

Heerema, E. (n.d.). *Alzheimer's prevention diet: 11 Tasty foods that reduce dementia risk.* Denver Health Medical Plan. https://www.denverhealthmedicalplan.org/blog/alzheimers-prevention-diet-11-tasty-foods-reduce-dementia-risk

Home Care Assistance Philadelphia. (2021, April 30). *5 Tips for family caregivers to get the rest they need.* Home Care Assistance.

https://www.homecareassistancephiladelphia.com/how-can-caregivers-get-necessary-rest/

How does dementia change a person's behaviour? Alzheimer's Society. https://www.alzheimers.org.uk/about-dementia/symptoms-and-diagnosis/symptoms/behaviour-changes

How to make your home dementia friendly. (n.d.). NHS. https://www.nhs.uk/conditions/dementia/living-with-dementia/home-environment/

How to read the "non-verbal" cues of a loved one with Alzheimer's. (2017, February 19). Anthem Memory Care. https://www.anthemmemorycare.com/blog/how-to-read-the-non-verbal-cues-of-a-loved-one-with-alzheimer-s

Kontz, J. (n.d.). *Coping with guilt as a caregiver.* Hospice Red River Valley. https://www.hrrv.org/blog/coping-with-guilt-as-a-caregiver/

Lecanemab approved for treatment of early Alzheimer's disease. (n.d.). Alzheimer's Association. https://www.alz.org/alzheimers-dementia/treatments/lecanemab-leqembi

Long-Term Care. (n.d). Alzheimer's Association. https://www.alz.org/help-support/caregiving/care-options/long-term-care

Maintaining your social life as a caregiver. (n.d.). The Holiday Retirement Community. https://www.holidayretirement.com/maintaining-your-social-life-as-a-

caregiver/#:~:text=Ensure%20You%20Schedule%20Social%20Ti
me,anything%20short%20of%20an%20emergency

Making your home dementia friendly. (n.d.). Alzeheimer's
Society.
https://www.alzheimers.org.uk/sites/default/files/migrate/down
loads/making_your_home_dementia_friendly.pdf

Managing everyday tasks as a person with dementia. (n.d.).
Alzheimer's Society. https://www.alzheimers.org.uk/get-
support/staying-independent/everyday-tasks-dementia

Mayo Clinic Staff. (2023, August 30). *Dementia.* Mayo Clinic.
https://www.mayoclinic.org/diseases-
conditions/dementia/symptoms-causes/syc-20352013

Mayo Clinic Staff. (2021, December 3). *Alzheimer's: Managing
sleep problems.* Mayo Clinic. https://www.mayoclinic.org/healthy-
lifestyle/caregivers/in-depth/alzheimers/art-20047832

Mayo Clinic Staff. (2023, August 9). *Caregiver stress: tips for
taking care of yourself.* Mayo Clinic.
https://www.mayoclinic.org/healthy-lifestyle/stress-
management/in-depth/caregiver-stress/art-20044784

Medicare Made Clear. (n.d.). *Does medical cover Alzheimer's
care?* UHC.com. https://www.uhc.com/news-articles/medicare-
articles/does-medicare-cover-alzheimers-care

Meditation tips for caregiver mindfulness. (n.d.). Voltaren
Arthritis Pain. https://www.voltarengel.com/supporting-
caregivers/meditation-tips-for-caregiver-mindfulness/

Memory loss and dementia. (n.d.). Alzheimer's Society. https://www.alzheimers.org.uk/about-dementia/symptoms-and-diagnosis/symptoms/memory-loss

Middle-stage caregiving. (n.d.). Alzheimer's Association. https://www.alz.org/help-support/caregiving/stages-behaviors/middle-stage

Mindfulness-based stress reduction for family caregivers of dementia patients. (n.d.). Warner School of Education. https://www.warner.rochester.edu/faculty-research/mindfulness

Mixed dementia. (n.d.). Alzheimer's Association. https://www.alz.org/alzheimers-dementia/what-is-dementia/types-of-dementia/mixed-dementia

Moore, W. (2021, November 18). *How to handle guild and other caregiving emotions.* WebMD. https://www.webmd.com/healthy-aging/caregiver-overcome-guilt

Muligan, C. (n.d.). *Quote by Carey Muligan.* BrainyQuote. https://www.brainyquote.com/quotes/carey_mulligan_425783

Newman, T. (2020, September 21). *Medical myths: all about dementia.* Medical News Today. https://www.medicalnewstoday.com/articles/medical-myths-all-about-dementia

NHS England. (2015, March). *Compassion in practice strategy and the 6Cs values.* England NHS UK. https://www.england.nhs.uk/6cs/wp-content/uploads/sites/25/2015/03/cip-6cs.pdf

Non-verbal communication and dementia. (n.d.). Alzheimer's Society. https://www.alzheimers.org.uk/about-dementia/symptoms-and-diagnosis/symptoms/non-verbal-communication-and-dementia

Noventi, L., Sholihah, U., Nurhasina, S., & Wijayanti, L. (2022). The effectiveness of mindfulness based stress reduction and sama vritti pranayama on reducing blood pressure, improving sleep quality and reducing stress levels in the elderly with hypertension. *Bali Medical Journal,* 11(1), 302-305. https://www.balimedicaljournal.ejournals.ca/index.php/bmj/article/view/3108/2034

Odell, C. A. (n.d.). How is life tree(ting) you?: trust, safety, and respect–the importance of boundaries. Stanford Student Affairs. https://studentaffairs.stanford.edu/how-life-treeting-you-importance-of-boundaries

Open Caregiving Team. (2022, January 2). Caregiver Therapy. Open Caregiving. https://www.opencaregiving.com/glossary/caregiver-therapy

Paying for care. (n.d.). Alzheimer's Association. https://www.alz.org/help-support/caregiving/financial-legal-planning/paying-for-care

Planning after a dementia diagnosis. (n.d). Alzheimers.gov. https://www.alzheimers.gov/life-with-dementia/planning-for-future#long-term-care-planning

Planning ahead for legal matters. (n.d.). Alzheimer's Association. https://www.alz.org/help-support/caregiving/financial-legal-planning/planning-ahead-for-legal-matters

Practical tips for supporting someone with memory loss. (n.d.). Alzheimer's Society. https://www.alzheimers.org.uk/about-dementia/symptoms-and-diagnosis/symptoms/memory-loss-support-tips

Quotes for dementia caregivers in need of inspiration. (2018, July 10). Active Pro Nursing & Homecare Inc. https://www.nursehomecare.ca/site/blog/2018/07/10/homecare-services-inspirational-quotes-for-dementia-caregivers

Repetitive behaviour and dementia. (n.d.). Alzheimer's Society. https://www.alzheimers.org.uk/about-dementia/symptoms-and-diagnosis/symptoms/repetitive-behaviour

Rohn, J. (n.d.). Quote by Jim Rohn. GoodReads. https://www.goodreads.com/quotes/7598940-one-person-caring-about-another-represents-life-s-greatest-value

Samuels, C. (2023, October 17). How much does in-home dementia care cost? A Place for Mom. https://www.aplaceformom.com/caregiver-resources/articles/cost-of-dementia-care

Schein, C. (2020, June 30). Providing compassionate care to your parent with dementia. Aegis Living. https://www.aegisliving.com/resource-center/providing-compassionate-care-to-your-parent-with-dementia/

Schempp, D. (n.d.). The emotional side of caregiving. Family Caregiver Alliance. https://www.caregiver.org/resource/emotional-side-caregiving/

Schulz, R. & Martire, L. (n.d.). XRX Florida: Alzheimer's disease and related dementias for specialized Alzheimer's adult day care, Level 1. A Train Education. https://www.atrainceu.com/content/5-stress-management-caregiver

Self-care for caregivers. (n.d.). UCSF Health. https://www.ucsfhealth.org/education/self-care-for-caregivers

Setting healthy boundaries as a family caregiver. (2020, April 29). Comparisons for Seniors. https://companionsforseniors.com/2020/04/set-healthy-boundaries-caregiver/

Short changed: Protecting people with dementia from financial abuse. (n.d.). Alzheimer's Society. https://www.alzheimers.org.uk/sites/default/files/migrate/down loads/short_changed_-_protecting_people_with_dementia_from_financial_abuse.pdf

Signs of caregiver burnout and how to prevent it. (n.d.). VITAS Healthcare. https://www.vitas.com/family-and-caregiver-support/caregiving/caregiver-life-balance/signs-of-caregiver-burnout-and-how-to-prevent-it

Six ways to ease caregiver guilt. (n.d.). McKnight Place. https://mcknightplace.com/six-ways-to-ease-caregiver-guilt/

Sleep and caregivers. (n.d.). Virtual Hospice. https://www.virtualhospice.ca/en_US/Main+Site+Navigation/Home/Topics/Topics/Providing+Care/Sleep+and+Caregivers.aspx

Smith, M. (2023, November 17). Caregiver stress and burnout. HelpGuide.org.

https://www.helpguide.org/articles/stress/caregiver-stress-and-burnout.htm

Staying connected–Caregiver newsletter. (2023, November 3). Caregiver Support Center. https://content.govdelivery.com/bulletins/gd/WAKITSAP-3794960?wgt_ref=WAKITSAP_WIDGET_80

Superadmin. (2018, July 18). Four tips for rekindling your social life as a caregiver. Lares Home Care. https://lareshomecare.com/four-tips-for-rekindling-your-social-life-as-a-caregiver/

The benefits of exercise and physical activity for caregivers and the individuals receiving care. (2020, February 27). Fitness for Health. https://www.fitnessforhealth.org/the-benefits-of-exercise-and-physical-activity-for-caregivers-and-the-individuals-receiving-care/

The Healthline Editorial Team. (2021, April 26). How to care for yourself when you have caregiver burnout. Healthline. https://www.healthline.com/health/health-caregiver-burnout

The importance of counseling for caregivers. (n.d.). Aging Care. https://www.agingcare.com/articles/counseling-for-caregiver-burnout-126208.htm

The power of active listening in interpersonal relationships. (2023, July 15). Zoe Talent Solutions. https://zoetalentsolutions.com/power-of-active-listening-in-interpersonal-relationships/

The progression and stages of dementia. (2020, October). Alzheimer's Society.

https://www.alzheimers.org.uk/sites/default/files/pdf/factsheet_the_progression_of_alzheimers_disease_and_other_dementias.pdf

Thirty-five quotes for caregivers that'll brighten your day. (n.d.). https://www.mycaringplan.com/blog/35-quotes-for-caregivers-thatll-brighten-your-day/

Tips for caregivers and families of people with dementia. (n.d.). Alzheimer's. https://www.alzheimers.gov/life-with-dementia/tips-caregivers

Vascular dementia. (n.d.). Alzheimer's Association. https://www.alz.org/alzheimers-dementia/what-is-dementia/types-of-dementia/vascular-dementia

Verbal and non-verbal communication tips for dementia caregivers. (2016, August 26). Samvedna Care. https://www.samvednacare.com/blog/verbal-and-non-verbal-communication-tips-for-dementia-caregivers/

Walker, T. (n.d.). Quote by Tia Walker. GoodReads. https://www.goodreads.com/quotes/888458-to-care-for-those-who-once-cared-for-us-is

Wandering in patients with Alzheimer's disease and dementia. (n.d.). UPMC. https://www.upmc.com/services/seniors/resources-for-caregivers/wandering-tendencies-patients-alzheimers-dementia

Weber, T. (2022, March 2). Setting boundaries as a caregiver is important for you and them. Human Resources. https://hr.uky.edu/thrive/03-02-2022/setting-boundaries-as-caregiver-is-important-for-you-and-them

What is Alzheimer's disease? (n.d.). Alzheimer's Association. https://www.alz.org/alzheimers-dementia/what-is-alzheimers

What is dementia? (n.d.). Alzheimer's Association. https://www.alz.org/alzheimers-dementia/what-is-dementia

What is dementia? Symptoms, Types, and Diagnosis. (n.d.). National Institute on Aging. https://www.nia.nih.gov/health/what-is-dementia

What is the role of compassion in healthcare? (n.d.). Point Loma. https://www.pointloma.edu/resources/nursing/compassion-healthcare

Wheeler, A. (2023, April 25). 5 Tips for providing compassionate dementia care. LinkedIn. https://www.linkedin.com/pulse/5-tips-providing-compassionate-dementia-care-wheeler-m-s-ccc-slp

Why is self-care important for caregivers? (2019, September 5). 24hour Home Care. https://www.24hrcares.com/resource-center/self-care-caregiver

Why self-care for caregivers is important for their mental health. (2017, June 13). High Focus. https://pa.highfocuscenters.com/importance-self-care-caregivers/

Zukav, G. (n.d.). Quote by Gary Zukav. BrainyQuote. https://www.brainyquote.com/quotes/gary_zukav_528235